Mini-Books are designed to
inform and entertain you.

They cover a wide range of
subjects—from Yoga to Cat-Care,
from Dieting to Dressmaking,
from Spelling to Antiques.

Mini-Books are neat
Mini-Books are cheap
Mini-Books are exciting

BYGONES: GAMES AND TOYS OF LONG AGO

is just one Mini-Book
from a choice of many.

Recently published in Corgi Mini-Books

BEAUTY AND YOU
A CAREER FOR YOUR DAUGHTER
A CAREER FOR YOUR SON
COLLECTING CHEAP CHINA AND GLASS
THE DIET BOOK FOR DIET HATERS
DRESSMAKING—THE EASY WAY
FLOWER ARRANGEMENT
GIVING PARTIES
HAIR CARE
HOME NURSING AND FAMILY HEALTH
INDOOR PLANTS
JAMS, CHUTNEYS AND PRESERVES
LOOKING AFTER YOUR CAGED BIRD
THE MAGIC OF HONEY
MONTH BY MONTH IN YOUR KITCHEN
NAME YOUR DAUGHTER
NAME YOUR SON
NO TIME TO COOK BOOK
SHAPE UP TO BEAUTY
YOUR WEDDING GUIDE
THE YOUTH SECRET

BYGONES:
GAMES AND TOYS
OF LONG AGO

Featured by Jean Morton
on ATV Television's programme
WOMAN TODAY

Researched and written by
CYNTHIA ROITH

Line drawings by Cynthia Roith

A MINI-BOOK BY CORGI/TV TIMES

BYGONES:
GAMES AND TOYS
OF LONG AGO

A MINI-BOOK 0 552 76395 0

PRINTING HISTORY
Mini-Book/TV Times Edition published 1972
Copyright © 1972 Cynthia Roith/Independent Television
Publications Ltd

Mini-Books are published by Transworld Publishers Ltd.,
Cavendish House,
57–59 Uxbridge Road, Ealing,
London, W.5
Filmset in Photon Times 10 on 9 pt. by
Richard Clay (The Chaucer Press), Ltd., Bungay, Suffolk
Printed in Great Britain by
Fletcher & Son Ltd., Norwich

CONTENTS

INTRODUCTION

Children's toys evoke the 'feeling' of each age with surprising accuracy. The other day I looked into the family toy-cupboard and immediately noticed the scientific toys; the 'astronaut' dressing-up costumes; and the 'world power' board games. Almost all the toys are made of plastic which, I suppose, is hardly surprising in this age of scientific advancement.

Today's children enact in their play the major world events that surround them, as well as the lesser daily happenings within the family circle. Play, to a child, is a serious business, as you can see if you watch even quite a small child playing a simple game of 'housekeeping'. The crying of a little girl whose mud pies have broken is just as intense as my own groans if I burn the roast beef! From an early age, when he clamours to clear the table or beat the eggs, just like his mother, a child's 'play' begins to teach him how to master new skills that will be of use to him in the next stage of his development.

At first, a toddler's play centres round family life; then when he starts to go to school, games expand to include 'bus conductors', 'shopping', and 'teachers'. Today's instant knowledge of current affairs through the mediums of radio and television, soon give him more exciting ideas to enact with his friends. For example, the world football cup matches; Sir Francis Chichester's voyage; Thor Heyerdahl's exciting expedition on 'Ra'; and the amazing buggy ride on the moon, all give growing children enormous scope for their imagination.

We can follow this up by looking at toys and games from any given age in days gone by and can thus easily sum up the type of life that was led at that time, and spot any exciting happenings that made special impacts on society. If we could look right back to pre-historic days, for instance, we'd expect to see sticks and stones used by the children, because we know how primitive life was in early communities. (An interesting point to note here is the similarity in this respect that pre-historic life shares with life in primitive tribes today in outlying parts of the world.)

If we could jump into a Victorian nursery we'd immediately sense the prosperity and stuffiness of the Victorian age, and see in the references to international trade and politics in geographical and historical puzzles and games, that communications and business were, by then, world wide. We'd also be sure to notice the *inventiveness* of Victorian toys; a reminder that in Victorian times, children were isolated from adults in their nurseries, and therefore *in need* of complicated and amusing toys with which to pass the time.

Primitive children lived in the heart of the family and were deeply involved in community life. Their sticks and stones, therefore, as well as reflecting the simplicity of the age they lived in, show that because they were never alone, and therefore never lonely or bored, they had no *need* for complicated toys.

So if we choose any culture or age at random, we can find out all about man's advancement socially and economically, just by peeping into the children's toy boxes, or reading their books. So many people collect old toys these days that one wonders if everyone has gone history mad. Or do we collect toys from a sense of nostalgia, yearning for the days when wars were localised and life was more secure than it is today?

CHAPTER ONE

DOLLS, DOLL'S HOUSES AND FURNISHINGS

It seems most unlikely that in primitive, pre-historic times, dolls, as we know them, existed. Certainly small carved and decorated 'people' *were* made, but these were idols, images of perhaps the sun-god or rain-god, and as such were certainly not for children to mess about with. They were too full of potent magic. Except in the case of the Hopi Indians of North America, who gave little carved and painted figures of the 'Kachinas' or rain-bearing spirits to their children, so that the children could familiarise themselves with these important gods. Primitive children, who wanted something to cuddle, were given a stick wrapped in a scrap of fur, or cloth. Features were never painted on these 'babies' because features (eyes especially) were associated with magic powers.

When archeologists found numbers of small terra-cotta 'dolls' in Egyptian tombs, they thought they had made great finds indeed. But then they realised that since the Egyptians believed in an 'after life', these 'dolls' were probably not children's playthings at all, but miniature likenesses of the dead people themselves, who in the after life would do any tasks required of the dead, on their behalf, thus leaving the spirits of the dead in peace. In any case, terra-cotta figurines would have been too fragile for children to play with.

Also found in these tombs were miniatures of everything needed for comfort in everyday life; furniture and jewels, etc. Looking at them, one can imagine them perfect for use in a dolls' house—but dolls' houses didn't exist in ancient

Egyptian times, and Egyptologists came to the conclusion that these miniature objects were for use in the after life too, by the tiny terra-cotta 'people'.

It's quite fascinating to examine very ancient things and to realise that centuries before civilisation came to Europe, the Egyptians not only had a very advanced culture and civilisation indeed, but had profound philosophical thoughts.

Of course, this is a subject far removed from the history of toys and games, so if these very short remarks on the subject whet your appetite, go to the British Museum's Egyptian rooms, where you can see what I'm talking about for yourselves, along with the make-up palettes, the mirrors, the hair ornaments, the wig-boxes, and even a perfect Egyptian wig, once used to beautify the rich in the age of the Pyramids and faithfully copied by specialist craftsmen to accompany them into the unknown after death. All this doesn't mean that toys didn't exist in Ancient Egypt at all, it just draws attention to the fact that what were once believed to be ancient Egyptian dolls and their accessories, turned out, on reflection, to be something quite different.

What of miniature figures unearthed from a *child's* tomb? Again, it's debatable whether such figures belonged to the living child, or were specially made to accompany him after death. There were, however, many other types of toys— such as board games, balls, and pull-along toys on wheels— but I'll talk about these later in the book in the appropriate chapters.

By Classical times, however, children's doll babies did exist, and looked pretty much as children's dolls do today. Pictured on Greek or Roman vases, there are countless dolls and they were often mentioned in the literature of that period. It was the custom for a Greek girl when she married to leave her outgrown playthings in a temple as an offering to the gods. And as Greek girls often married in their early teens, dolls were frequently numbered among the cast-off toys.

The dolls that have survived from both Greek and Roman times were made from either baked clay or carved wood. The clay dolls were jointed at the shoulder and thigh, so that the arms and legs could be swung up and down on metal pins; these would date from about the fifth century BC to the third century BC, but dolls were a little more sophisticated 100 years later in Rome, and if made of wood had joints at the elbows and knees as well, and looked very like the much later Edwardian 'Dutch' wooden dolls our grandmothers played with.

Since children and adults dressed pretty much alike in those days, the dolls would have been draped to match. Some of the clay dolls had 'built in' head-dresses which were just like adult head-dresses, and the carved Roman dolls sported the latest (carved) hair-styles. They must have been very elegant dolls indeed, even if they weren't comfortingly cuddly, and probably belonged to 'older' children. For the toddlers, dolls must have been made of cloth so that they could be dragged about, and sat on, and slept with just like modern toddlers' dolls. To bear this out, we know of a roughly tacked-together rag-doll that was found some time ago in Rome, in a small child's grave. It's very rare that cloth 'anything' should survive after hundreds of years, so this was a specially important find; proving yet again that children of all nationalities and ages have always responded to, and loved, the same type of playthings.

The earliest medieval European dolls we know about were German. and made from baked clay in little moulds. These were crudely made in comparison to the Classical clay dolls, because there were no separate joints at all. Legs and arms were moulded in with the bodies and quite immovable, and in fact these little dolls looked more like small statues for a shelf, than something to play with. Dolls like these would be carried from one area to another by peddlars who carried other goods as well. In England, in medieval times, it was difficult to get from one village or town to another, because of boggy ground or lack of decent roads. Towns were often isolated for months on end if the weather was bad, and it wasn't until the end of the seventeenth century, when draining of the English bogs and marshes began on a grand scale, that communications improved. This was hard on the peddlars doing a 'normal round', but they made up for it by attending as many local fairs as possible where they sold quantities of carved wooden dolls which they'd often made themselves.

The fairs were held on the local saint's days, and were attended by everyone, rich or poor, who could get to them. As well as things to buy, there were competitions—like the famous grinning competition where contestants stuck their heads through holes in a special board, and grinned as widely and as long as possible! There were things to eat like dolls made of gingerbread; and cloth and threads and musical instruments to finger and try. Traditionally, the special days in each area set aside for these fairs have come down to us as the 'half-closing days' of our local shops!

London's Bartholemew Fair at Smithfield dates back to the twelfth century, and sold boy *and* girl dolls, because it was as well known then, as it is now, that children of both sexes love dolls when they are very little. (Now-a-days, although we know this, we tend to give little boys golliwogs or teddy-bears instead of dolls, but if left to themselves they play with dolls quite happily.)

I don't actually know of any medieval or Elizabethan dolls in existance myself, and have always had to look at portraits or woodcuts to see what the dolls looked like. Medieval paintings were usually confined to religious subjects (illuminated manuscripts show us everyday scenes from medieval life), and it's not until the artist found a new role in society—that of the portrait painter—in the Elizabethan age, that we see pictures of stiff little English girls clutching equally stiff little dolls, alongside their stately parents.

English Elizabethan portraits are all of the nobility, who dressed the children's dolls as richly as they dressed the children, with bulbous sleeves and starched collars, and velvets from Genoa, and gold braids. These dolls were always called 'babies'. For some unknown reason, painting on the Continent was more 'free, and in the same period as the rigid (but charming) pictures we had here, we find the rolling easy style of artists like the Dutchman, Pieter Brueghel, who painted *peasant* children at play, and rarely painted the nobility at all. In the famous painting of 'Kinderspielen' finished in 1560 (Children's Games), Brueghel records a host of other children's games besides doll-games, including games that don't need toys at all—like 'leap-frog' or 'tag'.

In Germany in the fifteenth century, woodcuts recorded the same free artistic style, and showed in detail the famous carved wooden dolls of Nuremberg, a town that is still famous today as a centre for toy-making. Like the English Elizabethan dolls, these wooden (jointed) German dolls were elaborately dressed. Children were at this time dressed like miniature adults, so if dolls were dressed like the children, they ended up looking like adults too. A far cry from our own dolls which look just like babies and are dressed like babies. (I think the only modern exceptions to this are the National Costume dolls that are made for tourists to collect.)

By the seventeenth century, a new craze had swept Europe, that of collecting furniture, etc., for the new dolls' houses that were being made. The earliest dolls' house on record was the open-fronted house made for the daughter of the Duke of Saxony in 1558, and it was as playthings for the rich adult lady with time on her hands that these houses were at first invented. The sixteenth and seventeenth centuries were periods of increasing prosperity, and it became the fashion for ladies of the upper classes to spend their leisure and their money on collections of miniatures of all types. They called these 'toys', but to them, a 'toy' was not something to be *played* with, it was a collector's item, made of such fine things as silver, or even gold.

This collecting mania was especially strong among the rich burghers in Holland, who had made small cabinets to house their collections, rather like the furniture they used in their grand drawing-rooms, but with the cabinet divided into 'rooms' for display, instead of drawers or closed cupboards. At first only 'best' rooms were furnished, then it became amusing to furnish kitchens and laundry rooms, and soon tiny dolls were made to sit on the walnut chairs, or lie in the draped tapestry beds. This fad lasted until the beginning of the nineteenth century for adults, when commercially and more cheaply-made versions flooded the market and were given to the children to play with.

It must be remembered that children were only kept away from the original dolls' houses because these were filled with valuable miniatures. Occasionally, perhaps, an eighteenth century mama might let her little girl help in the polishing of the little silver candlesticks, but it wasn't until factory-made articles in tin and copper appeared on the market that mothers could let little girls play at 'house' all they wanted to, without fear of expensive damage, and the original houses were put away as valuable heirlooms.

In an eighteenth-century (adult) dolls' house, all the major changes on the scene of fashion were recorded faithfully—the cups were fragile Chelsea porcelain, the tea-boxes were made of tortoiseshell or ebony ... they obviously had never been intended as anything but luxuries for the woman 'who had everything'. As well as these gorgeous houses, separate but complete 'rooms' had been the basis for collections too, so that if you only wanted to collect 'drawing-room' items or 'kitchen' items, you could have had a fleet of drawing rooms or kitchens, measuring about 1 ft 6 in × 2 ft × 1 ft deep each, and looking rather like open boxes. Nuremberg was famous for making kitchens complete with brass moulds on the walls, kettles, pans, knife-grinders, graters, brushes and cutlery, meat-choppers and stoves. It would be extremely unlikely to ever get the chance to *buy* one of these early houses or rooms, they really are museum pieces and would be fabulously expensive.

But I suppose it is remotely possible that one could be inherited. I know one lady who is still living in the Victorian house her grandparents owned, which remains unchanged in almost every detail, who did inherit through those same grandparents, a lovely eighteenth-century doll's house on a stand. This particular one is like a grand red-brick Georgian house to look at. The façade, which swings open on two hinges has an 'Adam' fanlight over the front door and pillars either side of the door itself. Inside, the rooms have moulded ceilings and in some of the rooms, shreds of the original silk wallpapers remain in a delicate yellow shade. Yellow was one of the favourite colours of the late eighteenth century, and it is echoed in the yellow watered-silk dresses worn by the dolls who sit on tiny hand-made mahogany chairs.

Since the house was pretty complete when it was inherited, there's been hardly any recent additions in the way of furnishings, but the lady who owns it constantly goes to auction sales in the hope of buying bundles of really old material, and whenever she's lucky and comes across a piece of eighteenth-century silk velvet, or a scrap of genuine lace, she very carefully re-dresses any of the family of dolls whose clothes have gone rusty-looking with age. At one time, she said, she thought she'd add to the doll family and did in fact buy a 'grandfather' in a sale at Christies, but she had to give a lot of money for the doll—she was bidding against the museums—so she decided to renovate, rather than add to the dolls already in the house.

Unfortunately, even to buy dolls and dolls' furniture for *Victorian* dolls' houses, has become too expensive for most people these days, although Victorian dolls' furniture was machine made and was a reasonable price when it was actually fresh on the market, in comparison with the original houses which were filled with valuable miniature works of art. Long before Victorian times, adults had grown bored with the idea of dolls' houses for themselves and by the time Victoria herself was a little girl, sturdy nineteenth-century villas made of wood were being manufactured by the dozen. The little dolls that filled these particular houses had china heads, and the houses themselves were made at first with a simple upstairs and downstairs without any connecting staircase. By the end of Victoria's reign, there were usually six rooms in each house, including a below-stairs kitchen complete with buxom cook, and some of these houses were as big as a large chest of drawers.

My sister and I came across one of these later dolls' houses in a country auction sale about ten years ago. We bought it for ten pounds and excused our extravagance by telling ourselves that since we had five children between us, that worked out at only £2 per head, which by anyone's reckoning was cheap for 'a real antique!' Our house was in a deplorable state because it had obviously been stored in a damp attic, and all the wallpaper on the façade—made to look like pink bricks—and all the flowery, slightly gloomy inside wallpapers in plum and green and indigo, had gone mouldy, and it was obvious that it would all have to be peeled off and the wooden carcass of the house treated for damp.

We set about scraping the walls when we got home, with a kitchen spatula (which was nice and springy) and then we

wiped the whole house with malt vinegar which not only
kills any bacteria, but brings off an amazing amount of dirt.
(It works excellently on old furniture in the same way too.)
What a job we had to find something suitable to replace the
original wallpapers! Unlike old materials, which do turn up
from time to time in sales, genuine old papers *never* seem to
turn up and in the end, and feeling guilty because we weren't
restoring our house with genuine replacements, we hit on
the idea of handpainting a few yards of paper ourselves. I'm
supposed to be the 'artistic' one in our family, so for hours
—it seemed like weeks!—I scrunched myself up painting
tiny roses in a repetitive pattern on to plain cream-coloured
paper. When the paper was really dry, we cut it carefully to
shape and by turning the house on its back, side and front,
what seemed like a million times (no mean feat with a house
as big as a chest-of-drawers) we managed to arrange and
stick the paper in place.

We got very cross with each other and all the children
(who continually got in our way) that day! I came to the
conclusion that decorating houses—real or toy, was a sure
way to drive myself and all the family quite mad. But when
it was finished, our newly papered house looked beautiful,
and when I painted a growing trellis of roses around the
front door I began to feel pleased with life again. Our, by
now, very grumpy children sat in a gloomy circle to watch
this final effort and the eldest finally said 'Yes, but what are
you doing it all for?' (And in fact, we ended up by playing
with it ourselves, since Claire, our only girl, was a terrible
tomboy, and the four boys were on an anti-sissy campaign
that had begun months before, and actually, ten years later,
is firmly continued!)

By 'playing with it', I mean that for ten years now my
sister and I have had sessions of making and searching for
all the things that would fill a very respectable Victorian
middle-class house. We've been lucky and found tiny cane-

work tables and chairs in the Portobello Road for a few new pence, and we've been unlucky at sales and madly overspent on tiny brass beds. We've found that the best hunting grounds for fixtures and fittings have been junk shops in the North of England—because many of the huge old houses in the North are only just now beginning to be divided up into flats, or pulled down to make way for new estates. As these old houses get emptied, it's amazing what finds its way from the old attics and boxrooms into the local shops. I once found a complete set of small door-knobs in Birmingham for one pound, and another time came across a strip of Victorian tapestry work which was well worth the few shillings I paid for it, and cut up to make lovely 'best' carpets for the bedrooms and dining room in the house.

The actual 'people' for our house have been harder to find and inspired by the friend who inherited the eighteenth-century house I described, I've resolutely refused to make or buy modern dolls or reproduction furniture. Probably, the house will only really be complete by the time I'm a grand-mother! But whether it's ever completed or not, it has given and is giving me a great deal of pleasure. Collecting tiny things for antique dolls' houses can actually become a mania. On one of my searching trips I came across someone who had been collecting for twenty years. Only she's not content to collect for one type of house, she's set up four or five houses from different periods, in her living room, and spends a great deal of time and money trying to furnish them all, in period, and quite correctly. Eventually she hopes to give them to her local museum, hoping that they will prove to be valuable social history teaching aids for children. They certainly *amuse* children now, because modern children can't imagine the differences between tweeny maids and serving maids, and butlers and under-gardeners, and they laugh to see the footman's uniform, the minute warming pans, and 'papa' in his little nightcap with the roguish tassle. But because our children can't imagine the running of these old houses they don't enjoy *playing* with them nearly as much as they like their more modern toys, so it looks as if fashion has gone in a complete circle again, and once more dolls' houses are turning out to be collectors' items for adults.

As far as I remember from stories my grandfather told me, Victorian children were only allowed to look at, or play with, their dolls' houses on Sunday afternoons, or special days like birthdays. They actually had more real *fun* with miniature shops, and small butcher's shops with pretend joints of meat and a wooden butcher in an apron and boots, or a sweet shop with a tiny scales and jars and bottles of teeny sweets, were especially popular. When children play at shop today, they usually play with real tins of cocoa and custard, and real money 'like mummy', but in Victorian times, well-to-do mothers never went to the grocer—one of the maids did that—so the play was less 'real'.

By the Edwardian age, dolls for dolls' houses were made of continental porcelain, and the 'Dutch' wooden dolls which had been popular for over a hundred years had become more and more crude, as machines almost completely took over from men. (The first 'Dutch' dolls had appeared in the late eighteenth century, and had handcarved faces. The Edwardian ones had painted, instead of real hair, and set characterless faces.) No one seems to know why Dutch dolls are called 'Dutch', because it seems that they were originally made in Germany, and later on, like the little porcelain dolls, in Italy. Perhaps they got their name because so many toys were imported from Holland, that it was assumed that these dolls came from Holland too.

At Pollack's toy museum in London, you can still buy Dutch dolls for 50 new pence. They are about 8 in long. I bought one myself a week or so ago, and was asked to 'Please not give it to a little child as it was too fragile'—

which was true enough—and seemed to yet again bear out the theory that these dolls were kept for 'after Church on Sundays', when children were well supervised and on their best behaviour in the family drawing room. Let's leave miniature dolls now, with a reminder to see Queen Victoria's collection in the London Museum, and find out what was happening to bigger dolls in the eighteenth and nineteenth centuries.

Once again, those that have come down to us from the eighteenth, and the first half of the nineteenth century, are only the playthings of the rich. For when the Industrial Revolution started to gather momentum towards the end of the eighteenth century, poor children had no time for play when they were pushed into the growing factories to work. Play for them was an almost unknown luxury until well into Queen Victoria's reign, when the first children's homes and charity societies rescued hundreds of children and tried to ease their plight. But then they still only got second-hand toys at Christmas, if they were lucky (Victorian Christmas cards usually included a scene of 'charity-giving' along with a Christmas scene on the front), so most poor Victorian children never had 'Sunday' dolls at all, and never knew what it was to touch a doll with all her hair, and the blue paint of her eyes perfect and bright.

The most beautiful eighteenth-century dolls, like those in the Victoria and Albert Museum, had a thin coating of a type of plaster-of-Paris (known as 'gesso', and much used on finely carved eighteenth-century furniture as a layer), on their faces, which were then overpainted a soft pink. The white layer of gesso gave a delicate base to the pink paint, and gave a smoother surface too. Eyes were without lids and had finely arched eyebrows, and the dolls themselves had jointed wooden bodies and limbs. Sometimes wax was used for moulded heads which were fixed to both cloth and wooden bodies. Both types of these dolls had real hair,

dressed in the latest styles, sometimes powdered (if the doll
had been made before 1760), and sometimes unpowdered
and tucked inside a bonnet. Eyes were insets of coloured
glass. Although Queen Anne had died in 1714, these dolls,
all exquisitely dressed in popular styles from Paris, were
known vaguely as 'Queen Anne type'.

Sometimes similar dolls dressed in the very height of
Paris luxury were sent from France to guide the London
dressmakers, and be shown as models. These dolls were
called 'Pandoras', and when a new batch arrived in London,
advertisements sent all the most fashion conscious ladies
poste haste to their dressmakers to see them. These dolls
were bigger than the average child's doll, which usually
measured about 12 in from head to toe.

At the beginning of the Regency period, around the
1790s, we find muslin-clad dolls with stuffed kid bodies and
'Ascot'-type fine straw hats. These must have been much
softer to nurse, but I imagine that the delicate sprigged
muslin dresses got dirty very quickly—so perhaps, once
again, these are examples of dolls that children were hardly
allowed to touch! There was also a brief period around
1800 when very small dolls—small enough to stand on the
palm of your hand—were made completely of wax, in little
moulds. These were so fragile that very few exist today, and
they are rare collectors' items. They all have funny little
hollow red wax feet, cast in one with the rest of the doll.
And about the same time, papiermâché was introduced for
dolls' heads, but really only came into its own around 1870.
The centre of the paper trade was Wolverhampton, which
became the main supply centre.

The nineteenth century was an inventive time in all fields,
and we begin around 1807, to get dolls with eyes that open
and shut. (This was done by pulling a wire that stuck out
from the body.) Next, around 1830, we get the doll that
speaks—or rather squeaks—by means of a bellow arrange-

ment inside the body. Glazed china heads were by then the most usual and easily obtained, with extremely glossy black china hair, but around 1842, an *unglazed* very hard china ware was invented called Parian, which made even more beautiful and delicate dolls because it was so fine, It was also used for making delicate ornaments for the Victorian chimney piece. These dolls with china heads had cloth bodies stuffed with either horsehair or sawdust, and the china heads were cast all in one with neck and shoulders, so that the dolls could be dressed in décolleté if so desired. Their arms from the elbows down, and their legs, from the knees down, were also made of china. These china pieces had large holes in them where they were to be joined to the cloth bodies, and they were firmly sewn in place through these holes with stout thread. They usually measured about 14 in.

In the Great Exhibition at Crystal Palace in 1851, when all that was new and exciting in Victorian design was on view, a doll-maker called Augusta Montanari was awarded a medal for making a series of dolls with transluscent *wax* faces, hands and feet. These dolls had real hair and eyelashes (each was put into the wax separately), and the fine wax surface gave even more delicacy to the doll's features than Parian ware.

The firm of Augusta Montanari produced quantities of these dolls, with either jointed kid, or cloth bodies, between 1865–70, and in fact, in the 1870s dolls with wax heads almost completely ousted dolls with ordinary glazed china heads, although Parian ware from Germany remained popular. In other words, dolls with delicate 'cherubic' faces were 'in', replacing the more individual and 'peasanty' earlier dolls, and the slightly vacant and beautiful faces on the dolls was echoed in all the china figures and ornaments on sale in the shops.

It was a common belief that small Victorian children and their dolls looked (and should behave) like little angels, and even contemporary drawings show quite big children with wistful eyes and rosebud mouths. (Quite different from our own—more realistic—ideas, that children are usually scruffy, naughty, and tough!) Another variety of 'delicate' doll's head, which we mustn't forget here, was made by applying a wax coating on top of a hollow papiermâché head. These dolls were often dressed in National Costume (like the famous 'Welsh doll') and were made in great numbers around 1870. Although first introduced at the beginning of the nineteenth century, they are easy to date because the wax plus the papiermâché has, with the passing of time, crazed and crackled all over (due to the wax shrinking in the atmosphere, although the papiermâché underneath the wax has remained its original size). As on other waxy-headed dolls, these dolls had bunches of hair threaded into the wax with hot needles, and the bodies were fabric, stuffed, for preference, with sawdust. A few papiermâché heads without wax achieved a certain interest because they could be delicately coloured. The papiermâché was made in moulds just like contemporary papiermâché boxes, but these are rare enough to be museum pieces, and we are not likely to find one for sale anywhere.

Unfortunately, wax faces on dolls were easy to damage; any heat would melt them, and even a cuddle in bed with a small child could make the wax grow sticky and lose its fine detail. And the wax was difficult to clean. In London in the Pollock toy museum—as well as in countless dolls' hospitals up and down the country, there's a service which cleans these wax-headed dolls, and even threads hairs on to the heads again. I took a friend's wax-headed doll for just this service to Pollock's only a few days ago. The estimate was for a pound or so, but when the doll is returned to its owner, it will be as fresh as new, with long blonde hairs threaded into all the bald patches.

Another famous English wax-doll-maker of this period

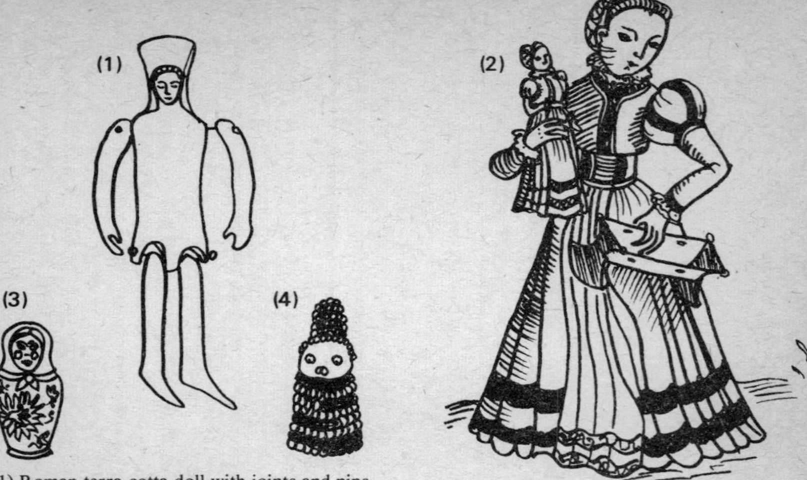

(1) Roman terra-cotta doll with joints and pins.

(2) From a woodcut dated about 1540; a little girl and her doll and its wooden cradle.

(3) Russian nesting doll, made of wood and brightly painted.

(4) A beaded Basuto doll to be carried by a small child. The beads are usually a mixture of red, white, and blue, and the doll's face made of black linen-like material.

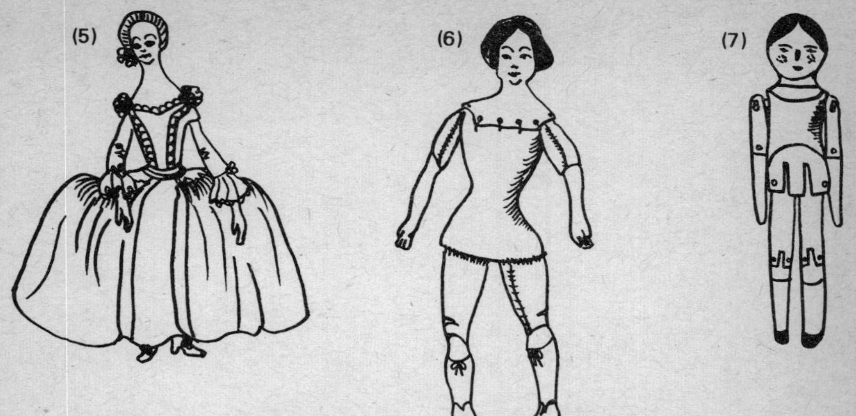

(5) English wooden doll with a wax head made around 1754; the clothes typical of 'Spring-time', with braid trimmings. Known as 'Queen Anne' type.

(6) Typical English doll of the 1860–80s. Limbs are china, fixed on to a cloth, sawdust-stuffed body. The hair on this particular doll is painted china, moulded in one with the head.

(7) Edwardian jointed 'Dutch Doll' made of wood.

was Mr. J. C. Pierott, who like Montanari was of Italian descent. Wax dolls were gradually replaced in popularity by dolls from Paris which had bisque-china heads. Bisque is rather like Parian ware, and is also left unglazed. These bisque dolls are easily recognised by their extra-large glass eyes, rather long noses and mohair wigs, and were manufactured by the Monsieur Jumeau, who had won a special medal at the Great Exhibition for the gorgeous dolls' clothes his factory specialised in. Jumeau dolls had at first kid-leather bodies, which were very tightly stuffed and had wires inside to keep the limbs stiff, but later, Jumeau dolls had wooden bodies, and finally, composition bodies with arms and legs joined by elastic (rather similar to many baby dolls made today).

Jumeau had great competition from German factories, who were exporting dolls with Parian heads to England in great quantities, so in order to combat this, he joined forces in 1898 with a fellow French doll-maker—a man called Monsieur Bru—who was becoming famous for his special dolls who all had slightly parted lips and huge round innocent eyes. Together they combined to produce dolls on a very grand scale indeed, but in spite of their efforts, Germany captured most of the late Victorian and Edwardian European markets, and German dolls—or the heads alone, which were fixed to home-made bodies—were on sale in England in some quantity, until the First World War.

About that time, bisque dolls fell from favour, to be replaced by rubber dolls, (first experimented with in the 1860s); celluloid-headed dolls; felt; composition; metal; and paper. Novelty dolls that walked, or could be fed, were in growing demand by the end of Victoria's reign, and between the two World Wars a new kind of novelty doll was invented—the cartoon and advertisement doll, like Micky Mouse, or Shirley Temple.

Dolls today are mostly made of soft but durable plastic, and have synthetic hair that can be shampooed and set. In 1890, a Tariff Act forced doll manufacturers to mark the country of origin of all dolls. This was placed on the back of the neck. The maker's initials, the name of the country of origin, a high number and a low number are all crowded together. The high number—it could, for instance, be 345, refers to the design number; and the low number, perhaps a $6\frac{1}{2}$ or a $7\frac{1}{2}$, refers to the size of the doll's head. Earlier nineteenth-century dolls often have maker's initials only, but if followed by E.E.P., the doll is 'registered' as having been made in France or Germany. Dolls made *before* the nineteenth century usually had no markings of any kind, so a visit to a local museum is a 'must' to check on the age and type of any unmarked dolls.

The book on dolls written by Gwen White lists several manufacturers and their marks, but a visit to a museum is a good idea whether you trace the correct mark or not. Perhaps *your* doll will prove to be rare, and usually only an expert can tell you if this is so, or not.

CHAPTER TWO

DOLLS' CLOTHES, AND PRAMS AND COTS

Although the last chapter was officially about dolls, lots of snippets about dolls' clothes crept in, because, after all, a doll without clothes is a very sad object indeed, and it's difficult to talk about one without at least mentioning the other. But in this chapter I'll go into the subject of clothes much more fully, so that if ever you are lucky enough to possess an antique doll, you'll know how to dress her.

First of all the golden rules for dressing an old doll is simply to dress her in something old. I've said this in Chapter 1, but can't emphasise enough that copies of old clothes, made of modern fabrics, just aren't good enough, especially as you *can* get pieces of genuine old material if you search around for them. Of course, one usually has to make do with modern sewing thread, so the true purist still won't be satisfied, but lots of Victorian sewing boxes still have original skeins of silk in them—I know several among my own friends—and since an awful lot of people have these old boxes tucked away at home, a little begging could easily result in the gift of a reel of thread, and the genuine flavour of the doll's original costume could be recaptured in detail.

Antique buttons are no problem—they are to be found in more junk shops and antique markets than I could name, and I know of one excellent little shop that sells nothing else, in St. Christopher's Passage, in London's West End. Jet buttons were all the rage in the late Victorian days, and silk-covered, pearl, or enamelled buttons, were popular in the eighteenth century. Braids and tassels, often of gold or silver thread, were known in England as far back as the medieval period. Gold braid was the first type of commodity available for buying by 'mail order'—in Elizabethan times—and goods were dispatched from London after selection had been made from sample cuttings. Delivery was notoriously erratic and slow, because bad weather often made roads impassable, and in any case, the roads were full of thieves and were unlit and dangerous. (Not until the first mail-coach service in 1784, was there a very *reliable* delivery service.)

It was in the medieval period, too, that loosely woven silk and silver threads—made into belts for rich medieval maidens—heralded the approach of the lace that was to prove one of the most popular trimmings of all time, and is still used in quantity today. Openwork weaves and gauzy linens had been known and loved in Egyptian times, but popular belief is that it was definitely the later medieval work that inspired late fifteenth-century workers in Italy and Flanders to work with needles and bobbins to make their famous edgings for dresses and caps. Many Dutch paintings of this period show how effective lace borders were on the dark dresses which were worn with simple, stiffened white caps.

By the end of the sixteenth century, lace was made stiff with starch, and fashioned into ruffs, as well as collars and cuffs. A picture painted by Cranach in 1540, showing the little Princess Marie of Saxony with her doll, shows lace trimmings on the sleeves of both the Princess and the doll, and the small lace ruff around the doll's neck heralded those grand tiered ruffs worn by the lady of fashion around the 1590s and 1600s.

The following centuries produced many lace designs of great beauty and delicacy, including among others 'Point de France' (often in the late seventeenth century incorporating designs of dancing girls and boys with birds and animals); Bruxelles needlepoint (heavy leaves on a fragile ground);

Venetian lace (with interwoven roses and stems); sprigged Alençon lace (with its background of rectangular mesh); and bobbin lace-work from as far afield as Milan (where gold and silver lace was made in the sixteenth century), and Flanders.

Henry VIII and Charles II both tried to curtail the importation of lace in order to give English lace-makers a chance to increase their trade, but they failed. Foreign lace was so popular that it was smuggled in, and in the late eighteenth century Flemish lace thus brought into England became known as Point d'Angleterre (English point-lace), so that it could be sold openly once it had reached English shores. Cromwell, too, tried to curtail expenditure on lace—as on other 'frivolities', and prohibited the use of lace while he was in power—a law that the poor classes adhered to, but which was ignored by the upper classes—and in fact also by Cromwell himself! And when Cromwell died in 1658, his burial costume was so richly trimmed with lace that it surpassed many Royal outfits! On the whole, English lace designs closely followed Flemish designs, and there's a wonderful display of these to be seen in the Victoria and Albert museum.

So you see, you must be careful, when dressing a doll, to get the 'trimmings' right. If in doubt, go to the National Portrait Gallery just off Trafalgar Square and study the costumes in the many varied portraits on show there. It is easy to be a student of fashion, because from Elizabethan times until well into the nineteenth century the artist fulfilled the role of today's photographer, lovingly and precisely recording people from all walks of life. In these old family portraits, every stitch and button and bow is recorded in detail, so there need to no problem about 'where to stitch the buckles?'

As for other fabrics—as a brief guide: silk velvets, brocade, and taffetas, often richly embroidered, were all the rage in medieval and Elizabethan times; striped and moiré silks were painted in imitation of fabrics from India in the late seventeenth century; sprigged printed cottons, and later, watered silk taffeta in yellows and pistachio green were popular in the eighteenth century; stripes appeared in Regency times; and marbled velvets, brocaded satins, glossy mohair, and woollen gauzes were worn by wealthy Victorians in an age when the textile industry was all agog with the first Singer sewing machines, and had never been so busy.

Quite enough choice to whet anyone's appetite! So, as I said in the previous chapter, since both children and their dolls were dressed like miniature adults until well into the nineteenth century, if you are lucky enough to possess or buy a really early doll you can copy the style of its clothes from any grown-up's portrait of the correct period. Baby-doll clothes on doll 'babies' only became the rage around the 1840s. Some people think this is because Queen Victoria had her own first child by then, and a wave of sentiment at the event swept over England, but whatever the reason, dolls from about that date can be dressed either as tiny adults *or* as babies, and be equally correct artistically.

Some of the baby dolls were almost as big as real babies, and if you find one of these, your problem for clothing it will be negligible. The fashion for wearing old clothes is so strong these days that markets like the Chelsea Antique Market and the Portobello Road (to name just two of the hundred-odd markets in England today) stock and sell huge quantities of Victorian clothes from baby bonnets to bloomers, and all you need is the stamina to push through the crowds to reach your goal—plus, of course, the money to spend!

Prices vary enormously, from 50 new pence for a ribbon-trimmed bonnet, to £30 for what is supposed to have been a baby dress (long, of course), worn by Victoria herself. I

bought a china-headed 1850-ish doll in the Portobello Road
for £5 a year or so ago, and she'd been re-stuffed so
violently that I had to unpick a seam and let some of her
sawdust out before I could get a baby dress to fit her! I
finally settled for spotted muslin with scalloped sleeves for
£2; a cotton petticoat for what would now be 50 new pence
(beautifully hand-tucked around the hem); a frilly bonnet for
30 new pence; and a pair of genuine soft leather Victorian
baby shoes for 10 new pence (that last was a real find!) So
for a total expenditure of about £8, I had a delightful
'heirloom' to keep in the family.

. It's incredible that every spot on the muslin has been
sewn on *by hand*, and around the scalloped sleeves a border
of satin stitch is so perfect it would even make machine-
stitching look lumpy. What amazing patience the Victorian
needlewoman had! I can imagine her, perhaps with little
round Victorian spectacles on her nose—sitting by the light
of a paraffin lamp in the family sewing room, and slowly,
slowly, stitching away at the new babies' dress. Outside,
might have sounded the clopping of hooves as papa came
home in a hansom-cab, and inside the house, kept warm
from coal kept in the new coal vases right by the fireside, the
new baby might have spluttered and cried in the nursery.

I truly think that a *real* babies' dress is by far and away
the most romantic of all the clothes a doll could wear! If you
don't agree, and want to dress *your* Victorian doll in more
grown-up clothes, base your designs on the Victorian adult,
or if it's a very late Victorian doll—perhaps a doll made by
Bru in 1890, with its round little (open) mouth, you'd also
be correct to copy children's Sunday-best clothes. Perhaps a
sailor costume, with knitted cotton socks and button-boots;
or a frilly broderie-anglaise dress (in maxi-length), with $\frac{3}{4}$
sleeves; tiny kid gloves and ruched bonnet. And don't forget
the underwear! By the 1890s little girls wore short, straight-
legged knickers that ended above the knee, instead of the

long pantaloons worn 30 years previously. (Until about 1780 no woman or child wore knickers at all, so don't worry about earlier dolls' underwear!) Little girls wore short knickers several years before their mothers—who around the 1890s were struggling with knickers that bunched around the knee, as well as hefty corsets that laced right down over the hips!

Dolls' prams and cots of the Victorian period are often found in the strangest places today—like chi-chi boutiques —where they are used to house pot-plants as part of the shop décor.

Some of the prams, like those that were imported around 1890, from the German area of Thuringia, have wicker-work bodies and white cotton hoods that can be lowered or raised by pulling a string. The wheels are metal—without tyres—and the whole pram has a very 'upright' look to it, as if the little girl who pushes it can only do so if her back is as straight as a ram-rod. (This 'upright-ness' was of course also characteristic of the real nursery prams made at the same date.)

Unfortunately, wicker-work is very susceptible to wood-worm. So if you manage to buy one of these particular prams (which will cost you today *at least* £20), please don't store it where there's the slightest suspicion of worm, or you'll see it powder and disintegrate almost before your eyes! Wicker should be gently scrubbed with a soft brush and rather dry suds if it's at all dirty—and after 80 years or so, it must be! Then it should be dried in the open air, if possible on the sort of softly, sunny, and breezy day that makes the most awful household tasks seem light and frivolous.

Other baby-carriages could be covered in leather, and I've even seen a 'country' Victorian pram made out of wood. The proportions of all these prams are quite different to those made today. Now, dolls' prams are low and rather wide, with plenty of room for two dolls to sit side by side, but Victorian dolls' prams were narrow as well as high, which sometimes made it difficult to tuck the covers under the hair mattress, so a sort of puffy eiderdown in a broderie anglaise cover which just lay on top of the doll and needed no tucking, often replaced ordinary blankets. The most luxurious of all dolls' prams had bodies of buttoned leather (just like Chesterfield settees), and fringed canopies on metal supports. These prams were 'back to front', so that the proud little girl pushed from a handle set behind the doll who could 'sit up and see where she was going'. This type of pram prevented her owner from looking (like anxious mothers do!), at her baby-doll's face all the time—but it meant she could watch the admiring looks of other little girls walking towards them, so possibly these particular prams were even more popular than the more usual types!

Rich little girls might put their dolls to bed, after their afternoon walk with their governesses, in brass or iron dolls' beds with horsehair-stuffed mattresses, very like their own beds. The beds, like the prams, would be rather high, so that if dolly could really walk, she's need to climb on a chair before she could jump under the bedcovers. These Victorian dolls' beds with brass railings and brass knobs are an absolute delight, although probably, like the grown-up's brass beds, they wouldn't be too comfortable. Posture-springing was unknown to the Victorians, and anyway it was considered more healthy to have a hard-ish mattress than a deliciously sagging and soft one!

Other Victorian dolls' beds were made of wood and had 'rockers' and this is a style we know children had for their dolls as far back as medieval times. But this was a more 'country' bed—on a par with the wooden Victorian dolls' prams, and, like all country things, untouched by high fashion, the style stayed the same for hundreds of years. Whereas in the same span of time in fashionable towns, dolls' beds—like the grown-ups' beds—changed considerably, from heavy four-posters to four-posters with slim carved supports, and from low straw-filled mattresses and embroidered linen hanging to high horse-hair mattresses covered with patchwork quilts.

CHAPTER THREE

TEDDY BEARS, GOLLIWOGS, MODERN ANIMAL TOYS, AND FOLK DOLLS

When 'Teddy-bears' were 'invented' they were the perfect answer to all the cries of little boys down the ages who had longed for a toy on which to lavish their affection. Dolls that little girls have always been encouraged to play with have, throughout history, been discouraged for little boys in case it made them too feminine. But we know now that both sexes need something to nurse and talk to when small, and boys (like girls!) grow out of this phase quite naturally when they get old enough to want to be 'just like dad' and turn to football and gardening. Little girls take longer to outgrow their dolls because their wish is to be 'just like mum', and mum is seen perpetually housekeeping and looking after the babies!

Anyway, all children find baby animals enchanting, and the fact that teddy-bears came into being because of a true story involving a real baby bear, made teddies very real to their small owners. And this is the story. . . . In November 1902, President Theodore (Teddy) Roosevelt went on a bear shooting expedition in Mississippi; came across a furry bear cub, and held his fire refusing to shoot such a pretty baby animal. He was photographed for the newspapers with the bear at his feet, and a leading American cartoonist, Berryman, drew a picture of the incident, called 'Drawing the Line in Mississippi'. The cartoon amused the public enormously and the baby bear became a sort of symbol of further Berryman cartoons.

As a gimmick, a Mississippi candy and hand-made-toy shop proprietor called Morris Michton, made a copy of the little bear out of golden brown plush, and the moment he put it on display, he sold it! He called it 'Teddy's bear' and as a demand grew for more of these cuddly and endearing toys, he wrote to Teddy Roosevelt and asked for permission to use his name officially. Permission was granted and the new teddy was soon the most sought after addition to any nursery.

At the Leipzig Fair, a few years later, a German teddy-bear was on display, made, along with other toy animals, by Margaret Steiff and her sister, who ran a small dressmaking or hand-made toy animal business. The teddies were a great success—several thousand were immediately ordered for the United States, and Margaret Steiff found herself involved in big business. English 'cut-out' teddies, to be made at home of soft flannelette, were on the market by 1909, and these had a certain popularity, although the original style of those ready-made in furry plush were always the most popular.

The earliest teddy-bears were tall and slim, in comparison to those made today, and were a yellow-golden brown colour. They measured about 8 in from the tip of their ears to their stitched toes. Today, they can measure $1\frac{1}{2}$ in, or be as big as a six-year old child and be made in brown, yellow, or even blue. They have been immortalised in books—(I'm sure A. A. Milne's Pooh Bear is the most famous teddy of all time)—and are frequently the only toy kept by adults as a souvenir of their childhood.

Whereas any dolls that may be kept—(and these are usually only kept because they were beautiful)—are carefully stored away in cellophane until a new baby girl arrives in the family, teddy-bears are often proudly displayed, and they are often taken to a young bride's new home, where they sit solidly on the best bedroom chair, a reminder of a happy childhood, and a symbol of good luck, security, and happiness for her new life. It is evident that little girls had the best of all worlds where toys were concerned, because although boys were weaned away from dolls and encouraged to nurse toy animals, girls were allowed to have animals *and* dolls.——And I've a sneaking suspicion that since dolls were fragile and teddies were not, teddies were always everybody's favourite.

The blue (nylon) plush teddy with golden-colour glass eyes that my own son was given as his first-ever toy was so loved by our dalmatian, that it was a perpetual tussle to keep it out of the dog basket! The first thing I did was to pull out the eyes on their dangerous wire stalks, and embroider eyes on 'Blue Teddy' instead. Ever afterwards, teddy's slightly cross-eyed look made him all the more appealing and amusing, and obviously even more lovable to the dog. Because, of course, being bigger than the baby (and weighing seven stone!), our dalmatian was a force to be reckoned with, and when he finally and irrevocably stole 'Blue Teddy' out of the baby's cot, and firmly sat on it, we gave up the fight. Ever afterwards 'Blue Teddy' went for walks with us held in the dog's mouth. We always afterwards wondered if our dog lacked security, and yearned for his puppyhood and the comfort of dog-family life in his old home near Tunbridge Wells!

Golliwogs first made their appearance in the 1890s in a series of children's books written in verse by Bertha and Florence Upton. The original golly looked almost identical to gollies still made today, except for one or two slight variations in his costume. The 1890 golly wore a stiff white collar with a red bow-tie above a *buttoned up* double-breasted blue jacket and plain red trousers. Modern golliwogs usually wear a rather short *open* jacket which shows a 3-button waistcoat underneath, and striped trousers with turn-ups. And usually his clothes are made of felt. In the

Upton book, Golliwog, 'a jolly dog', was always accompanied by his wooden Dutch-doll friends, and the biggest two had dresses with stars on a blue ground for one, and red and white striped cotton for the other. It was supposed that the stars and stripes dresses were made out of an American flag.

Golliwogs never quite achieved the same popularity as teddy-bears because they belonged more to the realm of fantasy, but they sold in pretty large quantities and still do. Perhaps *their* particularly endearing quality is their big round eyes which seem to look perpetually surprised, and which are almost hidden under a shock of furry black hair. Babies fresh from the bath often have the same straight sticking-up hairdo and the same astonished expression!

Dutch dolls, as I mentioned in Chapter One, had been on sale for quite some time before the publication of the Upton story-books, but the books recreated an interest in the dolls, and early Edwardian days saw a big increase in sales. (It is usually these Edwardian Dutch-dolls that are sold at Pollock's toy museum.)

The twentieth century has seen a spate of other stuffed animal toys in England often manufactured after the much publicised arrival of a new type of animal in the London Zoo (good salesmanship!). We've had the koala bear (though the ones made of real fur come from Australia and are not of English manufacture); the furry monkey with pink felt ears and feet; rabbits in striped trousers, and plump yellow furry ducks. Due to the influence of cartoon films in the last several years (the most important of which were made by Walt Disney), toy animals of this century usually have a faintly comic air. Donald Duck, for example, is a distorted duck with too-big feet and eyes; Pluto the dog has a variety of amusing expressions; the 'Jungle Book' animals are as individual as any human beings; and the 1001 Dalmatians look far naughtier than any real puppy could ever be. By slightly altering the size of one feature or another, Walt Disney has turned his animals into a whole troupe of real characters who are sad or happy, clumsy or wicked, and thereby infinitely appealing.

Folk-lore dolls can be as modern as a Walt Disney caricature, or as old as medieval times, although the term 'folk-lore' only appeared in 1846—relatively late in history. W. J. Thomas who invented the word, used it to describe 'the art of the unlettered', meaning the art of the peasant as opposed to the art of the rich. Some of the earliest woodcuts show peasants making toys of wood, and in fact wood figures prominently in most folk toys, since peasants tend to use materials near to hand and know next to nothing about importations of foreign fabrics or materials to use in their work. Clay is another material often used, and paper, if the toys came from the Orient. Like primitive paintings, folk toys have great charm, and would make a very colourful collection with the additional interest being its international flavour.

Folk toys from America include corn-husk dolls with faces painted with two rosy cheeks just like Edwardian Dutch dolls, dresses coloured red, and a baby in their arms; a hill-billy man on a straggly brown horse; and from Mexico, painted clay bulls or animals in papiermâché, bright and gay as the Mexican sun, with flowers painted all over them. From Russia, the most famous folk dolls are the 'Matrushka' nesting dolls with sometimes as many as thirteen in a set, and the famous Dymkovo whistles made to look rather like horses with strangely humped backs. These whistles were made of baked and painted clay, originally to be used in mid-summer celebration festivals for Yarila the Sun god, and the celebrations were so popular, that by the nineteenth century nearly all the local women were making dozens of whistles every week.

Amazingly, by about 1890, hardly any more whistles

were being made, and it's lucky that Yekaterina Denshina from Kirov took an interest in the old techniques, because her interest has caused a revival of what would otherwise have been a completely lost art. Also from Russia came the wooden bears that dance when a string is pulled, and wooden hens that peck their wooden perch when a weight on the end of a string is spun round and round. Often these particular toys are left unpainted, which I like very much, because in an age when most things seem to be made of plastic it's very pleasant to touch (and smell) natural wood. In comparison to modern plastic toys, these plain wooden animals are very cheap and are always stocked in really big toy shops; 'arty' gift shops; or foreign shops specialising in goods from overseas. The clay bulls from Mexico are not the only folk toys available in this country. Mexican dolls made of coloured straw, with straw crowns and wings (like the fairies on Christmas trees), can be bought in the Mexican shop in London's Lower Sloane Street, and so can pressed tin toys (mostly miniature kitchen tools); papier-mâché dolls painted a terra-cotta colour, with black hair and white socks; and brightly coloured humming birds.

From Africa come zulu dolls made from sweet corn-husks and clad in beaded hessian; and small black dolls only an inch or so high (made in Basuto-land). These dolls have round faces with beads for eyes and mouth, and elaborate arrangement of bead 'hair', and that's all! The head peeps out of a long neck completely covered with circles of beads in in bright colours, and there's no body, or feet, or arms! They are quite my favourite of all folk toys. . . So simple, yet the three white beads that mark the eyes and mouth give all the character these little playthings need.

The list of these traditional toys seems endless, but would not be complete without mentioning the gaily dressed minia-ture Indian men and animals made from lacquered wood. The men all sport fierce moustaches and their prominent eyes glare out from under dark arched eyebrows. Dresses for these little men are rather like coloured nightdresses covered with embroidered pinafore-dresses in purples and blues, pinks, greens, and yellows. And among the lines of animals march decorated elephants, some sporting a Howdah, like the processional elephants from the time of the Indian Raj. Japanese and Chinese folk toys are mostly made from paper, which was invented in China around AD 105, and immediately used for playthings (often, as in the case of kites, replacing silk and bamboo). Most Japanese and Chinese kite designs have special significance, like the Japanese carp fish kites. These were once upon a time flown outside the homes of small boys as a symbol of the struggle the boys would have in life, likened to the struggle of a fish jumping a waterfall. Kites first reached Europe at the end of the fourteenth century, and were shaped like large dragons. They were immediately popular, in spite of being cumbersome because of the heavy dragon's tail.

Today we've almost forgotten that kites were originally an Oriental toy, and on any windy day armies of men make their way to London's Hyde Park or Parliament Hill to compete with each other in flying oval, square, and diamond-shaped kites which are made of a variety of fine materials, as well as the original paper. The main thing *against* kites, as far as I can see, is that they cause untold frustration when they won't behave themselves. All around, one is sure to be surrounded by complacently successful kite-flyers of all ages, while one tangles oneself completely into an irritated monster—of all the traditional folk toys listed here, I'd put this at the very bottom of the 'present' list because of the special skill required. I personally much prefer my own collection of Russian bears that move. At least they work by the merest tweak of a string!

CHAPTER FOUR

TOY THEATRES, AND PUNCH AND JUDY, AND OTHER EUROPEAN PUPPETS

Everyone interested in toy theatres will be familiar with Pollack's toy shop, founded in the Victorian age and now lodged at 1 Scala Street, London, W.1. No. 1 Scala Street, is a funny little crooked London house, gaily painted on the outside; and inside, as well as finding fascinating reprints of Victorian toy theatres and character sheets for sale, one has the chance to wander through the rooms set aside as the Pollack Toy Museum and gaze at the sets of original miniature theatres, theatrical portraits, and a multitude of other Victorian games on display.

Pollack's toy museum was originally formed as a sympathetic background for the shop itself; is now an Educational Charitable Trust; and will, it is hoped, one day form the nucleus of a National Toy Museum in larger, more suitable premises. Bound up in the success of this particular shop is the whole story of the success and popularity of the Victorian theatre itself, so let us pause for a moment to study the situation of the theatre at that time. In 1840 there were at least sixty theatres in London, in comparison to the nine that were active around 1800. The most important of all the theatres were Covent Garden and Drury Lane, seating vast audiences (Covent Garden seated over 3,000), and claiming, under a grant issued in the seventeenth century by Charles II, that they were the only theatres at which plays with spoken dialogue could be performed. This amazing claim was upheld by the courts, and the remaining theatres had to 'make do' by presenting spectacles, circuses, and musical entertainments, minus the spoken word.

The law enforced the prohibition of dialogue at these spectacles so stringently that actors taking part were forced to strike extra-dramatic poses in order to convey their meaning to the audience; and placards held up on the stage had to suffice to inform the audience of any change of scene, or specially intricate details of the plot, since speaking was forbidden. Making 'musicals' became one way of side-stepping the law, and there were a spate of dramatic stories put into rhyme and turned into 'burlettas' or operas. Even Shakespeare became the victim of this type of treatment! But usually it was the practice to keep to dramatic spoken plays in the more important theatres, and concentrate upon spectacular effects, scenery, and music in the minor productions. Mass audiences became accustomed to enjoying a production solely on account of its colours and costumes, and even when the law prohibiting dialogue was abolished in 1834, it was deemed only necessary to have a minimum of spoken words to satisfy the audiences. The growing tradition of dramatic 'miming' adequately expressed the meaning of most entertainments, and the audiences demanded nothing further.

But instead of the small theatres, now given a free rein, putting on series of plays with long speeches, as staged in the major theatres, we find to our astonishment that at about this time there was a swing away from all spoken drama towards mere spectacle in the major theatres themselves. This might have been due to a wish to achieve similar successes in audience 'ratings', or perhaps it was because places like Covent Garden were so huge, most of the audience couldn't hear spoken words very well anyway, so that simpler dramatic techniques, as used in the small theatres, became expedient and even more effective than prose.

Victorian theatregoers had no compunction about throwing things at the actors if they couldn't hear properly, and it was easier for an actor to keep quiet and strike a dramatic pose than to receive a black eye from a well-aimed apple while pouring out a lengthy speech! In the early nineteenth century the most successful actors were members of the Kemble family, and Edmund Kean, and later, William Macready and Samuel Phelps. To have an audience boo and hiss one of their villainous roles was an achievement, proving that with the minimum of fiery words they had the audiences in their spell. Liston and Grimaldi were the comedians of the day, and Mrs. Siddons (a member of the Kemble family), the most popular actress. (It is at the very end of the Victorian era that Sir Henry Irving and Ellen Terry achieved fame.)

To suit the stylised presentation, stock plots and characters appeared in hundreds of different guises, and there was something satisfying in the predictable 'good triumphing over evil and living happily ever after'. Grimaldi the clown's famous pranks were legendary, and by the middle of the nineteenth century had helped a new type of adult entertainment to emerge—that of the slapstick pantomime, which has slowly over the years grown into the children's Christmas entertainment we know today. Principal boys and the Dame (impersonated by a male), made their appearance at the end of the nineteenth century, and by then contemporary melodrama depicting contemporary social situations, as opposed to traditional stock plays, was popular too, probably influenced by Dickens' observations and writings on the social scene. Quite lost in the robust nineteenth century pantomimes and dramatic plays, were the romantic ballets, fantasies and elegant speeches that had characterised productions of pantomime and theatre of the preceeding Georgian era.

The *English toy theatre* first appeared about 1811,

intended as a theatrical souvenir for theatre enthusiasts. At first, only sheets of paper, printed with pictures of characters out of various popular plays were put on the market. Writers like Dibden, Planché, and Fitzball had literally *hundreds* of their plays performed, and even Dimond and Pocock wrote thirty or so successful plays each, so you see that there was enormous scope for the sale of pictures representing a huge assortment of characters, and the pictures were avidly collected by regular theatregoers from the moment they made their first appearance.

The sheets were headed 'Characters in such-and-such a play, as performed at such-and-such a theatre', and under each picture was printed the name of each actor, and the part he played. The first sheets only portrayed the four most important people from each play; the next logical step was to make, as a more elaborate souvenir, sheets portraying *all* the characters. These in turn were followed by all the characters in all their changes of costume (with or without bonnet and apron, for example), and finally, all the characters in all their costumes and all the attitudes and emotions they showed on stage (in tears, fighting, horror-stricken, etc.). The sets of figures seemed to cry out for scenery, so plates of scenery were next made, and sold at the same time. They were accurately based on the actual scenes from each production, and cost 1*d.* if plain to be coloured at home, or 2*d* for a sheet already hand-coloured at the shops. The general feeling was that these souvenirs were too fragile and 'adult' for young children to play with, so it was usually the teenage boy in each family who cut out the characters and set up the scenery. In any case, the dramas depicted were not *children*'s dramas, and appealed far more to the adolescent and adult than to the toddler in the family circle. They were 'adult' or 'juvenile theatre souvenirs', rather than 'children's toys'.

The earliest toy theatre sheets we know about were

printed by William West, but by 1850 there were 100 active publishers; and by then the printed characters and scenery were sold together with scripts and plots, along with faithful copies of individual theatre prosceniums, drop curtains, and wire 'slides' to push the characters off and on stage while the dialogue was recited behind the scenes. One of the most famous of this army of publishers was Skelt, who made a speciality of buying up and reprinting, under his own name, stocks of engravings about to be destroyed by publishers who closed down. He was particularly successful, but had a great rival in J. K. Green. Green claimed to have been the real originator of toy theatres, but was never taken very seriously, as there was no evidence put forward to support this statement. When he died in 1860, a Mr. Redington bought up all his plays, which he sold in his shop alongside tobacco and haberdashery goods. It was in this shop that a certain young furrier, Benjamin Pollock, first met and fell in love with Redington's daughter Eliza. They married, and continued to run the shop after Redington's death. Ben Pollock gave up the fur trade in order to have time to print the scenes and character sheets that by then were selling so briskly, and in spite of the First World War, and the death of Ben Pollock himself in 1936, the family kept the business going until they were bombed out in the Second World War, and decided to sell up. Enthusiasm for Pollock's prints never waned.

Most dramas today either pose, and attempt to answer, a variety of theoretical questions relating to life, or are statements about life itself. They are far removed from the simple dramas of 'East Lynn' or 'The Miller and his Men'. The nearest we get to these plays, where there are goodies and baddies all easily recognisable by their costumes and the poses they strike, are the modern westerns. If you watch a crowd of children glued to the Saturday Western on television, and hear the roars as the hero overtakes the stagecoach, and the shouts as the villain tries to steal the gold from the mine, you'll have a pretty good idea of the reception the predictable Victorian dramas received. Our children *like* the Westerns to be predictable; they *like* to know at a glance who is on whose side—just as our grandfathers did. Half the fun in this type of entertainment is the 'letting oneself go' and shouting and clapping for all one is worth— something that organisers of sporting events have known right through history!

Out of the adult Victorian theatre has grown the tradition of modern children's entertainments like 'Batman', 'The Lone Ranger', and 'Aladdin', while modern theatre for adults has branched into something very different. A fascinating subject to explore! And by starting a family collection of Victorian theatre sheets, prints, and dialogues, you'll not only own some of the most attractive and amusing 'naïve' drawings and verses in existance, but you'll be well on the way to sharpening your enjoyment of every type of entertainment available today.

Puppet theatres have a long and interesting history, dating back to at least 500 BC when they were known and loved in Italy, Sicily, and Greece. They quite naturally followed in the tradition of the masked dramas of ancient Greece and often made use of the same tragic or comic figures. Apuleius wrote, in AD 200, that Roman puppets could roll their eyes as well as move their hands and legs. They were controlled by a wire attached to their heads, as well as by thin hand and leg strings, so although they could walk, dance, and run, their movements would be considered very stilted today, when puppets by means of a positive jungle of strings can move every eyelash and toe. And there were glove-puppets in these ancient days too, which were worn on the hand and had wooden hands and heads. Glove-puppet plays were performed by actors holding their hands above their heads in covered theatres.

The main difference between glove and string puppets, is that while string puppets can look and act just like miniature people, glove puppets not only look quite different but specialise in different actions, e.g. wielding sticks, pinching and poking, and crumpling up their 'bodies'. We know nothing about puppets of any type in the dark ages following the decline of the Roman Empire, but in medieval times they were an essential part of any entertainment put on by minstrels and jugglers, and travelled all over Europe with the performing troupes. By the seventeenth century, puppet plays, especially in Italy, had developed into elaborate dramas, and they were an integral part of the shows put on by the Italian Commedia dell' Arte when they crossed the Alps into France, or wandered into Germany, Holland, and Spain. The puppets soon acquired the same names and personalities as the Commedia dell' Arte actors themselves, and performed exaggerated versions of the same plays and mimes.

The French fell in love with the puppet version of Pulcinella, the shambling Italian peasant, who spoke in a squeaky voice, who was always found in the Commedia dell' Arte plays; and they produced their own version of this character, exaggerating all his physical characteristics, so that he almost became a cartoon-figure of the original hook-nosed, round-shouldered 'Servant from Naples'. And his popularity soon rivalled that of the Commedia dell' Arte 'Harlequin' (who became the string-controlled 'Jumping Jack').

By the end of that century, Pulchinella was the star of a number of plays written especially for him—'The Loves of Pulchinella', 'Pulchinella the Grand Turk', and so on—and took the role of compère or clown in every other popular play. He had come a long way from his humble peasant forefather, and was described as 'an eccentric grotesque', or 'a ludicrous hunchback' who could sing and dance and twist and twirl in a most endearing way.

The Italian puppet theatre crossed to England as part of the entourage of Charles II who had been exiled on the Continent during Cromwell's reign, and who in 1660 made a triumphant reappearance in London with great pomp and ceremony. Most of his exile having been spent in the courts of Holland and France, Charles was as familiar with the Commedia dell' Arte as he was with French music, Dutch fashions, or Italian wine. On October 8th 1662 the Italian puppet theatre performed at Whitehall before the newly established English Court, and Pulchinella was so well received that the Lord Chamberlain sent a gold chain and medal worth twenty five pounds as a reward to Pulchinella's performer—one Signor Bologna—for the pleasure he had given.

There was in England, however, great difficulty in pronouncing Pulchinella's name. And when, a little later, the character of the hunchbacked Pulchinella became so popular that he was included in puppet shows all over England, as a matter of course, various new names were tried out which would fit the English tongue more smoothly.—Punctionella was suggested; then Polichinelli; then Punchinello—until a drastic shortening of the name solved all the problems, and 'Punch' was born; soon to become a symbol of everything 'short and thick' like Punch himself. Puppet shows including Punch were as popular with the rich as with the poor, and Samuel Pepys frequently refers to outings he made in order to watch the puppets in their special theatres, in his famous diaries.

On March 20th 1667 he wrote that he took his wife 'to Polichinelli at Charing Cross, which is prettier and prettier, and so full of variety that it is extraordinary good entertainment'. And on April 8th of the same year he went to see a puppet show after being at the theatre proper and wrote that at 'Polichinello there had three times more sport than at the play'. By the end of the seventeenth century, toy puppet theatres, including 'Punch and his wife' were to be found in the children's nursery.

It is interesting to compare this with the fact that the other kind of toy theatres we discussed earlier in this chapter, were not only a much later 'invention' but were not intended for the nursery at all. *They* were, of course, flimsy paper souvenirs of adult entertainment, whereas puppets were strongly made of cloth and wood; they represented clowns and other characters known and loved by children from birth; and they could stand up to any amount of childish 'rough-and-tumble'.

Punch's scolding wife was given the name of Joan, and was dressed as a plain countrywoman. By the middle of the eighteenth century, she was having regular battles and quarrels with Punch (who was by now getting more and more 'English' and less French or Italian in looks and character); and Punch was given a variety of rhymes to speak which told the audience of his despair of her . . .

> *'Joan, Joan, Joan has a thundering tongue,*
> *And Joan, Joan, Joan, is a bold one,*
> *How happy is he,*
> *Who from wedlock is free,*
> *For who'd have a wife, to scold one?'*

is one song he sang in Fielding's 'The Author's Farce'. To which furious Joan replied . . .

> *'Sirrah if you dare,*
> *War with me (to) declare,*
> *I will beat your fat guts to a jelly!'*

She certainly didn't mince her words! Punch was more henpecked than belligerent—he usually only sounded brave when Joan had left the stage!

Strings that worked these puppets were still basically

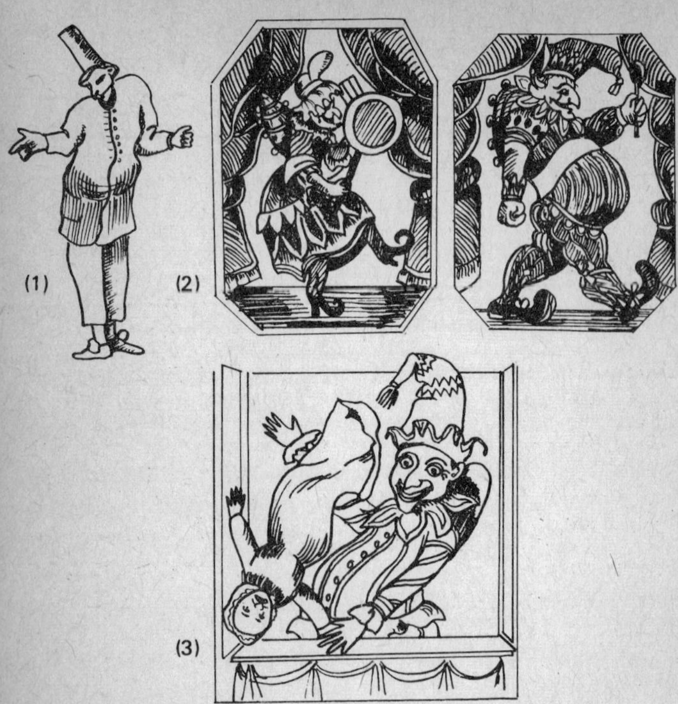

(1) The Italian Comedia del' Arte figure of seventeenth-century 'Pulchinello'.

(2) From two woodcuts of around 1800, of 'Punch and his wife Joan'.

(3) Punch throws his baby out of the window, 1840.

(4) 'Annette' in two poses from 'The Miller and his men', a favourite Victorian toy theatre play.

(5) A typical toy theatre set by Redington, around 1860.

(4)
(5)

simple, but there were a few sophisticated improvements, including a string attached to Punch's jaw to open and shut his mouth. (This had been introduced around the 1720s, when the successful puppeteer Powell put such a wire on to Punch for the first time, and a man in the audience declared 'that there is a thread (now) on one of Punch's chops, which draws it up and lets it fall at the discretion of the said Powell'.

The eighteenth century Punch must have found this refinement a great help when shouting at his wife! And the tin whistle held in the mouth of his performer made his shouting all the funnier as it came out in a squeak! By the end of the eighteenth century woodcuts show Punch with almost exactly the nut-cracker nose and chin, fat stomach, and hump that he has today, while Joan, brandishing a long-handled saucepan, dances after him in her mob-cap and panniered dress, a wicked grin on her sharp face. It seemed at one time that the close of that century was to see the last of dancing Joan and her husband, because as suddenly as they had taken Punch into their hearts a hundred years before, the public lost interest in all dancing puppets, and during the following Regency period it was the exception rather than the rule to find puppet shows at any of the Fairs. Travelling puppet-companies shrank in size, and often the puppet show was put on in the street, by a single man, who travelled the roads with his booth and puppets on his back. Hand-puppets replaced the wooden figures of 2 ft high or so, that had warranted the proper stage of the 1700s, and the elegant eighteenth century puppet theatres with their galleries, boxes, and pits (there were about four in London around 1760), fell into decay.

It was to everyone's astonishment that these street booths slowly but surely began to draw the crowds again, and find a new place in the hearts of the people. Punch as a glove could dart about in a way the large old string-puppets on a stage had been unable to do, and the proximity of the watching people to the little booths, gave opportunities for back-chat with the audience that everyone found hilarious, and a soon 'indispensable' part of the show itself.

In 1841 the little fat puppet achieved immortal fame when a new satirical and comic paper was called *Punch* in his honour, and by this time Joan had mysteriously changed her name to Judy, and they had acquired Toby the dog. This version of Punch has never fallen from favour, and is as much a part of the modern holiday scene as lettered rock, seaweed, and shrimps. He can be seen along with the other Victorian puppets who were his sturdy companions 100 years ago, in the London Museum; and anyone who wishes to study his history further can follow up their museum visit with that fascinating book called simply 'Punch and Judy', recently written by George Speight. Artists like Cruikshank and Rowlandson have made innumerable drawings of the puppet booth and Punch in action, and their cartoons are echoed in this short, immensely amusing, and perfect rhyme written in 1826 about Punch and his grumbling wife:–

'And now they hug—now fight—now part—now meet,
While unextinguished laughter shakes the street.'

No other puppet can claim such a long and varied career, although there have been other celebrated puppets, like the Italian wooden marionette Pinnochio, who is a relatively modern addition to the puppet scene. And of course we cannot leave this story of European puppets without sparing a thought for the puppet theatres of the Orient, where puppets were often made with papiermâché heads, or were completely flat, as the shadow puppets of Java. But their evolvement is, indeed, another story.

CHAPTER FIVE

SOLDIERS AND FORTS, AND GAMES IN BOXES AND ON BOARDS

In 1650, at the age of twelve, the son of the Dauphin Louis XIII of France received from his father a set of over three hundred silver toy soldiers, which had once belonged to the Dauphin himself. They were used to teach the boy the tactics of warfare, with the aid of real gunpowder and a fort built of earth in the Palais Royal Gardens, and became not only a favourite toy but a valuable part of the young Prince's education. Until about 1800 all toy cannons used powder, but changed to spring action power after that. But to make soldiers out of a precious metal like silver is quite exceptional. The usual metals have always been tin or lead, pewter or scrap alloy. A small percentage have been made in Germany, Africa, India, and Birmingham, out of copper. And around the time of the First World War even aluminium had its day, sometimes being salvaged from wrecks of the huge silent zeppelins.

The earliest record we have of toy soldiers being made of any metal is from the thirteenth century. A flat tin model soldier of this date was found in the River Seine, and is especially interesting because it is also one of the earliest records of this particular type of toy in existence at all. The real heyday for toy soldiers began much later, in the eighteenth century, when the exploits of Frederick the Great inspired toy-makers to make models of his armies and his enemies, so that his victories could be relived and re-enacted at home. Father as well as their sons have enjoyed setting up and collecting toy soldiers ever since.

At first the toys were made in low relief and looked rather like gingerbread men. They were actually made in similar moulds. The moulds were made of slate and the metal used was either tin or pewter. The most famous family for producing these funny little flat men who looked either grimly ahead, like their horses, or had their heads set sideways, was the German Hilpert family. They were tin-smiths who moved to Nuremberg around 1775, and although their soldiers have brought them the most renown, they also made a flourishing business out of making, in the same type of moulds, tin animals, gardens, and furniture. All their figures and animals stood on little flat bases, and measured just under 3 inches. Intaglio carving inside the slate moulds gave detail to the figures when they were cast. Their tin monkeys were especially amusing with careful carving in the moulds, giving great detail to the wizened 'monkey-faces'. Soldiers were given 3-D beards and moustaches in the same way.

Seiffen was another area famous for tin-mining and toys, and the whole Nuremberg and Seiffen areas were at this time also making quantities of wooden toys. Miniature wooden soldiers were among the great variety of assorted playthings, but seem, once they were used and soiled, to have been thrown away. They were relatively cheap, and therefore easy enough to replace. So although we know they were made, there are none remaining that can be examined and collected today, whereas lead and tin soldiers having lasted rather better, can still be found. By the middle of the nineteenth century the making of toy soldiers and wooden forts, had become an increasingly important part of the toy industry.

In England, one manufacturer was making more than two tons of scrap metal toys (including soldiers) a week, and in Nuremberg, a standard 30 mm height was being established for the still flat soldiers, by the firm of Heinrichsen. French solid lead soldiers began to be made in the round, and were a welcome change from the 'flatties' from Germany; and the step that followed, the production of *hollow-cast* lead figures, (invented in England by William Britain—a very patriotic name!) ensured that England was kept well to the fore on the international toy market. These hollow-cast figures were economical to make, and were sold in sets in shiny red cardboard boxes, the painted soldiers being fastened with a thread of cotton to a strip of card, which kept them neatly in place.

In the little book *Floor Games* by H. G. Wells, he wrote the following paragraph about toy soldiers . . . 'They used to be flat, small creatures in my own boyhood, in comparison with the magnificent creatures one can buy today . . . Now they stand nearly two inches high, and look you broadly in the face, and they have the movable arms and alert intelligence of scientifically exercised men. You get five of them mounted or nine afoot in a box for tenpence-halfpenny.'

Buglers and cavalrymen, tiny guns and standard-bearers all had their place in the Victorian games of war. The main problem was how to store the little figures, once the 'armies' grew too big for their original cardboard boxes, and the problem was finally solved by making wooden forts with large hollow stands. The stands were painted to look like the approaches to the fort; had sloping 'roads' leading up them to the fort-entrances; and could form an empty storage place by swinging the complete fort open on its hinges, away from the stand itself. When it was closed, the fort clipped shut on to its base with a simple curved metal catch. The forts were all made to look like fairy-tale palaces, with turrets and archways and courtyards. Often, the turrets and gateways were removable (they fitted back into position with a pin) and could be stored if necessary, in the stands, along with the soldiers and guns. The forts were painted in bright colours. But soon printed paper façades made their appearance on forts from Thuringia, in reds and yellows and greens and greys, and they made a gay contrast to the stands which were usually painted dark-green or brown, and had pseudo tree-bark stuck on to them to resemble rough ground or rocks.

I bought one of these Thuringian forts about six years ago, for £2, in a junk shop in the Harrow Road. Today, it would easily cost £10, and the earlier hand-painted forts, approximately double. The base of our particular fort measures about 18 in by 14 in, and is roomy enough to store over fifty soldiers and their equipment inside. Soldiers can ride up the sloping pathway, across a flat wooden drawbridge (which can be raised and lowered) and enter the fort's courtyard through a crenelated arch. Each wall of the courtyard is covered with grey and red paper marked out as blocks of stone, and little shuttered windows, and on top of each wall, in each corner, stands a removable turret with a pointed red roof, which is fixed on to the wall by the simple means of a little sticking-out pin that slots into a round hole in the appropriate position on the brickwork. Each turret is of slightly different size and design, so that the fort can be made to look a little different each time it is played with, by the simple method of changing the turrets around. And the archway can be changed with a massive door, and one whole wall, with a horses' stable block.

When we first bought the fort, we spent a whole afternoon changing and then changing again, the positions of the turrets and the walls, and found we could either get a grim and bleak 'prison' effect, or a fort that looked ready to haul out its celebration flags and bang off its guns after a special victory, with all its little red shutters turned outwards towards the approaching armies. We've been lucky enough to find several lead soldiers of that exact period, although prices have risen so sharply in the last five years that we've now ceased our searching. At the time we bought the fort we spent about £6 on an assortment of men and animals, including a pair of lead donkeys carrying the parts of a cannon on their backs, and a red-cross wagon drawn by four horses and accompanied by four men in special uniform. The wagon is very like the wagons used in blazing a trail across America in the days of the Civil War. It has a flat base big enough to carry at least four 'wounded', and the hood can be raised or lowered, or lifted right off the wagon. Both the hood and the wagon itself carry the sign of a red-cross in a white circle, and inside the wagon, a tiny wooden box contains minute scissors made of tin, and a roll of linen bandage.

Today, I'm sure that the same amount of money would only buy one splendid item like this, instead of the several we were able to get. I'm afraid that although the fort is still being used, the original soldiers and equipment we bought have been locked away, and modern plastic toys have had to take their place.

Victorian toy-cupboards were full of toys in boxes, some of them purely pleasurable like the soldiers, and others highly educational like most of the board games or jig-saws available. The earliest jig-saws were known as 'dissected maps' and were an entirely original 'educational' idea of Wallis & Son, the mapmakers, who first put them forward in the 1770s. Wallis & Son were also printers of historical and religious books, and soon the 'map-jigsaws' were followed with hand-coloured Biblical scenes, or scenes of great battles, to be followed by scenes from everyday life. The jig-saw became a normal part of Victorian nursery equipment, and often an object of dread to the children, who were already suffering under a surfeit of other games that made them 'think'. Geographical and historical jig-saws were often 'played with' immediately before the nursery governess gave a geography or history lesson, so they were never regarded as 'fun' in the way we look at them today.

Unfortunately, games cease to be amusing if they impart

great slabs of knowledge; anyone who is in the mood for a jig-saw or board game is very rarely in the mood for a combined lesson on imports, boundaries, and exports; and so the Victorian jig-saw, although sold in quantity to parents anxious to educate their offspring, was usually received with gloom and depression in the nursery.

As collector's items, however, they are splendid, if only as a record of place-names and political affairs long past. And anyway, however dull they might have been, they were certainly attractive to look at with their soft hand-done colours, and decorative lettering. Everyone who collects anything at all will agree that collections must be attractive to look at, as well as interesting, or one loses interest in the collection very quickly. It's certainly true that not everyone has the same idea as to what is beautiful, but in the case of these mid-nineteenth century jig-saws, I've never yet met anyone who has failed to find them visually pleasing.

Other 'boxed' toys were equally attractive, and equally boring! The variety was bewildering, and covered approximately the complete syllabus of an elementary school. Card games were often banned because of their scandalous passions for gambling (in all forms, but *especially* with cards) in the preceeding Georgian and Regency periods, that had ruined the grandparents of many fond Victorian papas. *They* had no intention of allowing their sons to get a taste for betting like those 'wicked and wasteful Georgians!' So more or less the only card games allowed were played with packs of picture cards, and not with ordinary cards at all. For instance, 'Snap' was played with a series of cards showing cartoons of everyday situations with snappy captions underneath. 'Who would be a doctor?' was printed under a yawning man with mutton-chop whiskers, a night-shirt, and candlestick; and 'Oh, you monster!' under a snake glaring eye to eye at a whiskered Professor. The game was played in the same way that we do now, with excited shrieks as matching cards were turned up. 'Happy Families' had cartoon families dressed in contemporary costume. One late Victorian set has a Mrs. Bones the Butcher's wife, looking suspiciously like the character in Alice in Wonderland (first published in 1865) who 'beats her baby when he sneezes'; while Miss Bones her daughter sits gnawing a bone while dressed very much like Alice herself. Of course, games like Faro (or 'Pharoh', the game that made Count Rostof lose a fortune in Tolstoy's *War and Peace*); or Whist (from which descended that most intellectual card game in the world, Bridge); or Poker (Queen Victoria's favourite); were all well known. But any child who wanted to join in a betting game like these had to sneak down to the servant's quarters and play there!

It's not difficult to recognise a genuinely old pack of cards. Cards have been around a long time—at least 600 years in Europe, and longer in the Orient—and standard patterns and sizes have always made them easy to date. 'Tarot' playing cards were the earliest known in Europe and came from Italy. In medieval times they were very popular for fortune telling. Cards have traditionally always been made of paste-board (the paste makes them opaque, but some medieval Tarot cards were made out of ivory. A typical Tarot set consisted of twenty two picture cards depicting a fool, plus twenty one allegorical cards, numbered, and showing with each number a virtue or a vice. All the pictures showed full-length people with their heads at the top of the card, and their feet at the bottom.

By the fourteenth century, an additional 56 cards (divided into 4 suites with 10 numbered cards and 4 picture cards in each suite, in the way of Ancient Chinese packs), were added; thus making each Tarot set a massive 78 in number. The original picture Tarots then became trumps. These early sets were all laboriously hand-painted, and were either square or very thin oblongs, or, most rare, round.

Some were enormous, and measured 6 inches by 4, and they were all extremely expensive.

In the fifteenth century, pictures were wood-engravings and the colours were put on with stencils and dyes; but not until Thomas de la Rue was granted a Royal patent in 1832 and began extensive designing with lithography, did cards become relatively inexpensive. He made popular the lacquering of cards. All this time cards had been left with plain backs, as gamblers felt that patterned backs would be too easy to 'mark' and cheat with, but around 1850, geometrical patterns began to appear. By 1870, court cards were double headed so they were right whichever way they were turned (medieval-style full length portraits just vanished), and they were dressed in the style of either Henry VII or Henry VIII. Corners, which had previously been squared off, were then rounded, and corner indexes became standard. Modern cards are a standard $3\frac{1}{2} \times 2\frac{1}{2}$ in, or $3\frac{1}{2} \times 2\frac{1}{4}$ in, and they are sometimes made of acetate cellulose (plastic); are die cut, and have scraped and sanded surfaces, with lacquered and gilded edges. Quite easy to distinguish from larger, squared-off old cards. The British Museum has a very important collection of playing cards, and rules of games like Tarot, Pharoh, Whist, and Rook (yet another old favourite), can be found under the name of each individual game, in the *Encyclopaedia Britannica*.

CHAPTER SIX

WOODEN TOYS

Besides the several wooden folk toys I described in Chapter Three there's an army of other attractive wooden toys which can roughly be divided into two groups—the indoor wooden toy —and the toy more suitable for playing with out of doors. If you yearn to be a collector of toys and are amazed at the prices old toys sometimes fetch in the auction rooms, you'll do well to concentrate on collecting toys made out of wood, because these invariably cost less than more exotic playthings, and have a charm all of their own. Indoor wooden toys, like Noah's arks, are often composed of 'families', which can be added to at any time, are fairly small, and being unbreakable don't need any special 'care and repair'.

Like early wooden dolls, most European wooden toys come from the Nuremberg area in Germany, just as, after the end of the eighteenth century, tin toys came from the German tin-mining area around Seiffen, and late nineteenth-century Bisque dolls came from Thuringia. Industrial development in the late nineteenth century changed the character of the previously hand-made toys to some extent, by making them less crude and more commercial, but the industry continued to flourish until the First World War put an end to all exports from Germany for the time being. The majority of wooden toys one can find in old shops and street markets today, date from the late Victorian and Edwardian periods, so I shall concentrate on these.

Many are copies of toys available to children as far back

as the fifteenth century, but the earlier prototypes are normally only found in museums. Humming tops, hobby horses, skittles, and hoops are typical 'outdoor' examples. Playing Cup-and-ball (or Bibloquet as it was called in France), swept across France in the seventeenth century, and became such a mania that just about everyone carried a set as they went about their daily business. Popularity for this game of skill was revived in the Victorian age, and nearly all Victorian families had at least one in the nursery. The object of cup-and-ball was to flip the wooden ball, which was attached to the cup by a string, into the cup itself. The cup had a handle which was held in the hand. The art is to flip the string firmly but not too hard, otherwise it might swing round and rap the knuckles!

A more harmless toy—but one only suited to children this time—was the Hobby horse. This is undoubtedly a descendant from the branch-held-between-the-legs as a make-believe animal to ride, enjoyed by children in primitive societies, but by the fifteenth century had proper horses heads. Victorian hobby horses sometimes had a wheel attached to the stick 'body' of the horse to help it along the ground as the small child galloped about, which the fifteenth-century horses lacked. Otherwise, they were almost identical, both having charming, rather than fierce, expressions; hairy manes; bells that were attached to leather reins; and rather round eyes. The Victorian stick bodies were usually gaily painted blue or red, whereas the early horses had plain unpainted wood.

Victorian children might have enjoyed an occasional gallop, but without doubt preferred rocking horses, which were far less hard work! Rockers were probably inspired by hobby horses, but made their first appearance far later; the earliest known rocking horse having belonged to Charles I, when he was a little boy. This particular toy can be seen in the Antique Hypermarket in Kensington High Street in

London, and is a very rough and ready version of the glamorous horses seen in the nineteenth and twentieth centuries. There's something extremely romantic about seeing a toy that once belonged to a famous personality, but unfortunately, romantic or not, particular toys like these cost far more than their contemporary copies because they are unique. Stories of Charles I usually dwell on his entanglements with Parliament, and I must confess that until I'd seen his rocking-horse I'd never really thought very much about his boyhood. Life as the son of James I must have been at times both dangerous and embarrassing, but James I was a man of culture (in his reign began the now world famous English Royal art collections); and cultured men usually have an interest in their children's pastimes. So perhaps it was James I himself who designed his little son's horse, and was the first person to lift him on to it, and show him how to set the rockers in motion.

By Victorian times the rockers were strongly arched strips of wood, and the horse itself was really lifelike. Perhaps it might be a 'dapple-grey', with dilated nostrils, real horse-hair or mohair mane and tail, and often a beautifully polished leather saddle. Sometimes they were nearly half life-size. The Charles I horse and rockers are 'all in one' in the sense that the rockers are made of planks of wood solidly leading up to a roughly carved saddle. The horse's head and neck grow out of this solid block and lack most of the details that make a horse look 'horsey'. There are no ears, for instance, and no nostrils at all. No proud, haughty look. These refinements first appeared towards the end of that century, and successive craftsmen exhibited their skill until in the beautiful Victorian models they reached the height of achievement.

A Victorian rocking horse today, in good condition, could cost £50 or more, which would make it a luxury addition to any home, where once these horses were a normality. Today's versions lack all the fire and detail of those made a hundred or so years ago, and although they certainly rock, mass production has made them poor, dull descendents of their vigorously carved great-grandfathers.

Small wooden horses were always included in any 'set' of wooden toys, and are often the only animal missing, because Victorian children loved these little horses so much they often carried them around in their pockets and subsequently lost them. And if, as in *early* Victorian times, a little girl's pocket was like a separate bag tied under her dress and around her waist with ribbon (this is how Lucy Lockett lost *her* pocket!), one can easily imagine the toy horses, plus any other small treasures getting mislaid!

Realistic little animals of all kinds were made in natural spruce and imported from Germany in the 1840–1900 period, along with little Bavarian chalets, dovecots, and fir trees, sold as farm-yard sets, and 'hunting' sets and Noah's arks, and Christmas crib scenes. Drawings of these sets were laid out in pattern books, so it was easy to repeat the most popular orders. The trees and gate-posts were all carefully turned on a lathe much as the seventeenth century toys had been, and they were sometimes painted in bright colours, and sometimes left quite plain. All the sets came in matchwood boxes, with the animals carefully fitted head to tail inside, which was one way of teaching small boys and girls to be tidy! Modern German wooden farm-animal sets or zoos, or collections of boxy little houses with onion-shaped roofs which make up into little 'towns', come in net bags, and cost surprisingly little. They can be found in the Galt or Abbott educational toy shops, where enlightened toy producers and designers have realised that these simple and solidly made little toys are much safer and stronger than most of the cheap plastic and metal toys on sale.

A complete Victorian farm or zoo would these days cost at least £15, but a relentless search in all the local junk shops would probably produce a good number of single Victorian animals, each costing only a few new pence, which, since they were made to a standard size, can very successfully be grouped together, and if necessary, repainted to 'go' with one another. This is the sort of collection any small child will happily help with. My elder son and I once made a lovely collection of animals, which he carefully painted to match one perfectly preserved toy cow we bought from an old lady in Brighton. That was twelve years ago. Since then, the same collection has been enjoyed by all the other children in our family, as well as the children of three more families, and when last seen, was still going strong, and visibly growing!

There are several books in the libraries which show in detail the colour schemes of these Victorian toys. Perhaps the nicest is the book devoted entirely to German toys, called *An Illustrated History of Toys*, in which the coloured photographs show very clearly exactly how you can copy the flowers or spots on the many little carved animals and people.

Boxes of wooden bricks came from Germany in the 1880s, complete with a few sheets of suggested 'castles' or 'towns' that could be made from the bricks. The lids of the boxes slid off to reveal a beautiful selection of triangles, oblongs, arches, and squares fitted together as carefully as any jig-saw. I bought such a box for the equivalent of 50 new pence a few years ago, which was so perfect that I'm sure it had never been used, and I thought it remarkably cheap because whereas modern wooden animals are *inexpensive*, modern wooden bricks are always costly, and a similar *modern* box of two hundred assorted bricks would at that time have cost me at least £3. Originally, boxes of these bricks cost 6*d.* up to £5, according to size. Square wooden alphabet blocks and blocks that when put together made up maps of the world, or just attractive pictures, are still to be found today, although a perfect box would cost about £5. These 'picture' blocks would be called jig-saw puzzles (as I've said in the last chapter), but of course were very simple, the pictures being usually made up of only 36 blocks, whereas jig-saws have now anything up to a thousand or so pieces, and are designed for adults as well as children.

All these boxey games are remarkably 'collectable', are splendid amusements for all the family on wet Sunday afternoons, and can happily be stored in any corner of any cupboard. But before leaving boxed-games, I must mention the nesting blocks (square blocks without one side that fit inside each other), that the American Charles Crandall invented around 1870. These are still made today, and are recognised as being classics among children's toys, and are to be found in every nursery and nursery school. Crandall also invented bricks that could slot into each other instead of just being balanced *on* each other, and out of this idea grew his boxes of wooden, painted acrobat figures which can be slotted into each other to build up into pyramids. In the Bethnal Green museum in London, a similar Victorian toy called 'John Gilpin' is composed of a wooden Gilpin and a jointed wooden horse, which can slot into each other in at least eight different ways, as illustrated on the sheet of directions that went with the toy. From this 'slotting' idea, other firms made up sets of a variety of subjects—perhaps the most famous of which is Shoehut's Humpty Dumpty circus. Made in many sizes and exported from the States, it was a huge success over here, and if pieces got lost they could be ordered again through Selfridges.

Victorian penny toys sold at fairs (often costing *more* than a penny!), included acrobats of wood on wooden stilts, who jerked when the stilts were squeezed together; and whistles; and wooden Harlequins, who danced when a string was pulled (just like the folk Russian bears). Harlequins were based on the early Italian comedy figure, and were

(1)

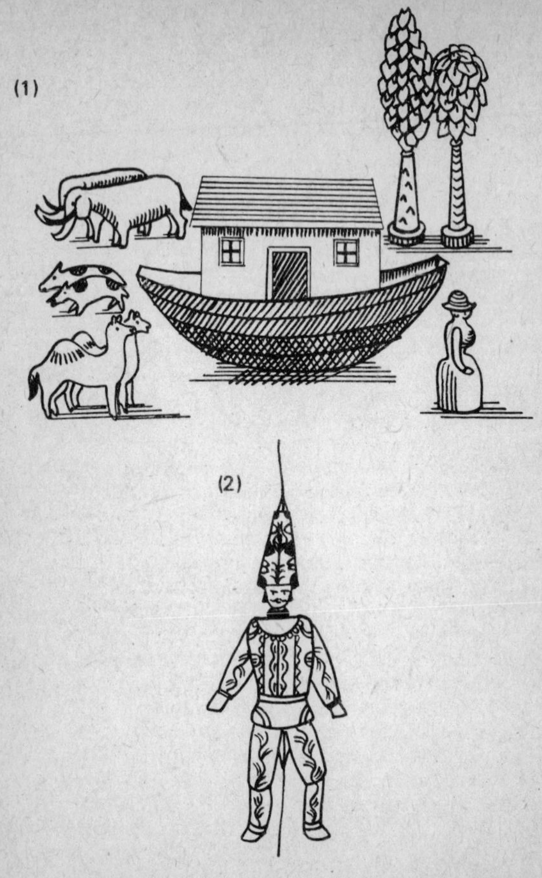

(2)

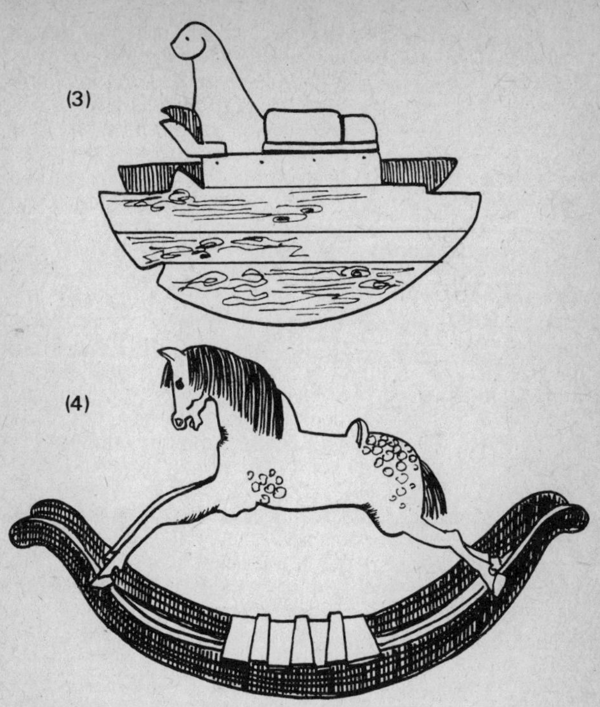

(1) Nuremberg wooden Noah's Ark, trees, animals and Mrs. Noah.

(2) French 'Jumping Jack'.

(3) Charles I's wooden rocking horse.

(4) Rocking horse made in England around 1800.

copied in porcelain in Meissen, Dresden, and other leading
European factories also. Harlequins were once called
Jumping Jacks and first made their appearance in France
around 1746. The craze for playing with these dolls affected
adults as well as children (just in the same way as the game
of cup-and-ball), and these funny toys became so much a
part of life that police banned them, fearing that constant
play would cause women to give birth to children with
twisted limbs like the toys themselves!

Nineteenth-century Harlequins were made in both
America and Germany, always with a painted costume of
diamond-patterns, although originally the dolls had been
painted with squiggles and stripes. Other cheap Victorian
wooden toys were also with movable parts—it was the
movement that 'sold' the toys in the first place—and a
collection of these which include wooden bees on expand-
able wooden scissors; wooden monkeys on sticks; and bears
hammering on pegs, can all be studied in the famous Pinto
collection of wooden bygones. The lists of wooden 'indoor'
toys are endless and in fact I've only given a selection of the
most popular ones, because of lack of space. I'm sure that in
your searches you'll come across many that I haven't mentioned at all! This is part of the fascination of collecting toys
of any sort. You think you've established a fairly comprehensive collection, when, wham! something quite new to
you comes to light in your aunt's attic, or the local antique
shop.

But no chapter on wooden toys would be complete
without a mention of toys meant to be played with *out* of
doors. The origin of some of these goes right back into
antiquity, like whipping tops, yo-yos, hoops, and skittles.
Hoops were actually first made of metal in Ancient Greece
and Rome, but from the width of hoops shown in sixteenth-
century paintings, it seems certain that by then, hoops were
made of springy wood, just as they are today. Tops, in

ancient Egypt were made of hard glazed composition, but by 1340 at least, were made of wood and often 'whipped' by a whip with a double tail, as we know from the illuminated manuscript *The Romance of Alexander*, of that date. It's possible that tops from the Orient reached Germany in the early 1500s, and tops were popular here in the eighteenth century, as we know from Parson Woodforde's diary. In the Victorian age, they were in as much demand as yo-yos (first depicted on several classical Greek vases) which disappeared after Classical times, and re-appeared here at the end of the eighteenth century, introduced into England via the Far East.

Glazed clay made the earliest known nine-pins in Ancient Egypt, but once again, wood became the 'usual' material as years went by. The original 'pins' were shaped like the minaret domes on the Brighton pavilion, but the passing of the years gradually altered this, too, and Victorian nine-pins were more like turned wooden sausages, about six inches high. Perhaps the change had been brought about because tall slim 'pins' were easier to carry than the original stumpy ones. This, at any rate, would seem a logical conclusion. Sometimes the pins were fashioned to look like soldiers on parade.

The most interesting of these outdoor toys is to my mind the pull-along toy, which dates right back to 1000 BC. In the British Museum is a toy wooden tiger made at that time in Thebes. His eyes are glass, his teeth are bronze, and he opens and shuts his jaws by means of a string that goes through the hinged lower jaw, and comes out at the top of his head. He measures about 6 in long, and stands in the same case as a toy I liked even more (although this particular toy was not to be pulled along). This was a wooden mouse with long tail and, again, a mouth that opened and shut via a string. The tiger from Thebes had no wheels (presumably he was just dragged), but by Classical Grecian times there were plenty of wheeled toys, like the toy cart painted on a fourth-century Apulian water jar. (Earlier Greek toy carts had been made of terra-cotta, and glazed.) The stiff wooden horse on four wheels was the usual Victorian version of the English push and pull toy, but on the Continent the toys were often given other animal heads, like that of the goat. Funnily enough, modern push-toys are more likely to be dogs, though I have recently seen a series of furry donkeys with long eyelashes being wistfully inspected by some toddlers in Harrods!

CHAPTER SEVEN

PAPER

Paper was invented in the Far East by the Chinaman Tsai Lun, in AD105, although the Ancient Egyptians were writing and drawing on sheets of papyrus (a type of paper) as far back as 1800 BC. But as far as we know, papyrus was never used for anything as frivolous as toys. While paper very rapidly became the usual medium for toys like kites (previously made in the Far East out of silk).

From the East, too, came, via seamen and travellers, the art of Origami, or paper folding, which became one of the arts of the English Victorian fairground. At home, Victorian ladies made Origami flowers to decorate the house, and it's a curious fact that although in England we've always preferred to work with plain white paper because it was cheap, in Japan, where this art originated, coloured paper was more usual. (Only around 1860 did English *coloured* paper become inexpensive.) By the First World War, Origami aeroplanes were being made as a hobby by both men and boys; and as a craft it enjoys enormous popularity today, with books and television programmes giving ideas and directions for making the most elaborate designs. These, and the craft of paper-sculpture, make very good displays for shop windows. Origami is an inexpensive hobby, but it does require a fair amount of patience. If you are interested in learning more, any good stationers can provide a cheap booklet illustrating simple designs, together with a sheaf of special coloured paper. Not just any paper will do. It has to be a certain thickness and smoothness, or the designs 'flop'. But given the correct type of paper and a few diagrams, it's really quite easy to produce traditional shapes like the old French 'Cocotte' (chickens), or more abstract designs that can be used in Christmas tree decoration. Other folded paper amusements coming from Japan include 'magic' tissue-paper flowers, that burst open when put in a glass of water, and reveal minute exotic flowers.

However, these folded treasures apart—what amusements has paper offered to children in the past? Immediately, one thinks of books—but I want to lay these completely aside, except for the cut-out toys that were on sale with books (which I'll talk about in a moment or two)—and concentrate on flat separate *sheets* of printed cut-outs that were so much in demand a hundred years ago. The art of printing came into England from Germany in the mid-fifteenth century (we were at that time writing laboriously on vellum); German books printed in this period used ink on carved word-blocks. Later, separate letters in frames made printing much easier, and one set of letters could be combined in many ways and used for quite different books once their original purpose had been fulfilled.

Caxton set up his famous printing press in Westminster in 1476—and Caxton Hall is still famous, although nowadays used quite differently. By the sixteenth century, Germany was still leading the way in printing (and this time, with pictorial sheets that were made to be cut up and stiffened, so that figures and animals could stand on a table). The printing was thick, so that the sheets closely resembled wood-cuts, and included sets of 'everyday animals' like donkeys and dogs, which could be collected into little farmyard sets. The animals were usually between 1 and 2 in high. These were followed with 'PROTEAN' dolls, plus a variety of clothes, printed and all ready to cut out, on single sheets. The dolls were named after the Classical demi-god PROTEUS, who changed his shape at will.

By the eighteenth century, France was successfully turning out sheets of cut-out dolls' house furniture and armies of soldiers; and at the end of that century, interest swung to England, where the new 'movable' cut-out paper dolls were selling like hot cakes. There were sheets of cut-out Jumping Jacks, Pantins, and Pierrots, too, that could be made to dance just like their wooden counterparts, by the addition of a piece of fine string. These dolls came complete, with changes of clothes. Until the 1850s, when the trade reached its peak with machine-coloured lithographs, all the pictures were coloured by hand. Easy enough to spot, as hand-colouring always includes some thick and some thin streaks of paint; some splodges; and some mistakes; whereas machine colouring is uniformly neat and flat. By then, sheets from Denmark and Austria were on the market; and Epinal in the French Vosges, was emerging as the leading French area. 'Imagerie d'Epinal', eventually came to mean simply, 'Made in France'.

Lace paper and tinselling spread from Germany (where it had been used as early as the seventeenth century on religious sheets); and became almost an English hall-mark, destined to appear on most Victorian popular printing including the new Christmas cards and theatrical portraits. Sheets of Columbine and Harlequin, or Pantin, or indeed almost any subject, measuring from an inch or so square to over 18 in square, can be bought for as little as 25 new pence in London's street markets, and make very decorative pictures if simply framed and hung on the wall. You can, of course, cut them up and make the designs of dolls or ships or houses as directed, but I almost feel this would be a pity, and would certainly never cut any sheets I owned myself.

If you look at the sheets on sale in places like the Portobello market, you'll be astonished to notice the serial numbers. One design I looked at was numbered well into the 8,000s, which indicates that an awful lot of different patterns were printed. As for the printed sheets of cut-out dolls sold in combination with stories for small children—they were a great success from the moment they appeared which was in the early nineteenth century Regency period. The little books and the cut-outs were sold together in little thick paper wallets. The stories were about little girls called Fanny, or perhaps Phoebe, and for every scene that unfolded in the story, little Fanny or Phoebe had a costume, which could be cut out and fixed to cover her. In this way, the stories were brought to life for little girls, and the cutting out trained their fingers to manipulate a scissors carefully—a most useful accomplishment in a century where every girl had to learn crafts like dressmaking or embroidery as a matter of course. Little Phoebe was a 'cottage maid' . . . and . . .

> *'Where'er she left her humble cot,*
> *She never pass'd unheeded by,*
> *And though arrayed in plain attire,*
> *She drew the traveller's wand'ring eye.'*

Cut-out pictures of the 'plain attire' and the cottage maid herself, made Phoebe more real than many other childish heroines.

By the end of that century, both the Americans and the English were producing sheets of incompleted pictures, which could only be completed by the addition of cut-out figures fitted on to the blank spaces; and the French were making complete cutting-up books instead of single sheets, which could make whole villages, complete with mountains and fir-trees. Pasteboard architectural models, like churches or temples, were complicated and precise to make success-fully, but were in demand to go with the complete villages. Easier to make, and therefore *more* in demand, were gipsy caravans, carts and other vehicles. (This particular craft had a history dating back to the time of Defoe, but only reached peak popularity when the books of villages, etc., I men-tioned above, came on the market.)

MECHANICAL TOYS AND MAGIC LANTERNS

This chapter will deal with perhaps the most fascinating of all toys—those that move. We've already talked about moving toys like Jumping Jacks and Puppets, and seen how they enjoyed enormous popularity from the moment of their first appearance. But they relied entirely on the personal contact of a manipulator to bring them to life and breathe personality into them. Without this 'human touch' they were poor, inert, lifeless creatures—and perhaps the secret of their popularity lay in this very dependence on their owners—they became, so to speak, *part* of their owners.

Now the toys I'm about to describe were fitted with mechanisms that made them move quite independently once they had had their initial switching on, or winding up, seen to, and maybe it was because they were independent that they were never regarded with the same affection as the puppet-type toys. Except funnily enough, when their mechanisms broke down. When this happened, fond care was lavished on the broken parts. Perhaps when they were perfect they were *too* perfect, which made them seem remote from the real flesh and blood child.

Anyway, whatever the reason, it is an established fact that adults have always loved clockwork and electric trains, and mechanical dancing dolls more than their children did; while children have always preferred the puppets who 'needed' them. Having established that, let's look straightaway at the toys that flooded the markets around the 1860s, that were powered by clockwork or steam. This doesn't mean that this was the date they were invented—on the contrary, clockwork toys had been in existence since the seventeenth century, but in those days they were the expensive playthings of the rich, and were often made of precious metals (as were the earliest dolls' houses and accessories); and it was only when the nineteenth century was well advanced, that this type of toy became cheap enough, and made in enough quantity, to be given to children for fun.

Most of these nineteenth-century toys were made of tin, although lead was sometimes used for decorations, and they were all hand-painted. The majority came from the Nuremberg area in Germany, but France and America and England had expanding business too, and one country often influenced another, as the growing international marketing scene came to mean exchanges of ideas, as well as exchanges of goods. The clockwork dancing dolls were often only a few inches high, and were modelled in the round, with their mechanisms hidden from view under their tin skirts, or in the seats of their chairs. They might hold a kitten, or a doll in a basket, and they were dressed just as real little girls of the 1860s, with ribbons in their hair; little bonnets; frills on their sleeves; and rosettes on their shoulders—all, as I've said, made of tin.

One especially pretty model I've seen shows a dear little girl in a long dress, with a bustle bow, dancing with a boy who is clad in a sailor suit. He wears the floppy beret with streamers; the bloused top; and the little heeled boots that were fashionable at that time; and they spin slowly round and round when the machine, hidden in the little girl's skirt, is wound up. They do not dance to music . . . they just dance. *Musical* dancing dolls were usually French fantasies —which I will discuss later in the chapter. Another model, which might appeal more to a boy, shows a very serious young man riding a huge three-wheeler bicycle. At that time three-wheelers were often ridden by grown-ups (although now they are normally for small children); and had three wheels of equal size. (The Victorian child's three-wheeler sometimes had a horse's head instead of a normal straight handlebar, and might even have a horse's saddle to sit on, instead of the curved metal support that had to suffice the adult). On this particular model, the mechanism is placed between the two back wheels, and the rider crouches over the handlebars. When wound up, he pedals furiously, and it's interesting to note that the pedals are placed on the front wheel itself, and not, as we are used to, in the half-way position between the front wheel and the back. Another point of interest is that the model is dressed in a cloth outfit—and from that we can deduce that he was more expensive than the little dancing tin sailor and his girl. In fact, he cost 3s. while the tin soldier model cost only a few pence. But his striped red and white trousers and blue cloth jacket make him look a real 'swell', so probably he was worth the extra money! Today he'd sell for several pounds whatever his condition, and one would be extremely lucky to find him at all.

A great favourite in America at about this time was the clockwork picture, again descended from the elaborate 'toys for adults' of the seventeenth century. Driven by a miniature steam engine, one picture shows a violin-playing cat, whose head and right arm move once the machine is started; while three little kittens with their hands (paws!) on their hips, dance a little jig. Actually, since the jig only appeared in 1872, I suppose this particular picture must have been made after this. Other pictures, equally attractive, show a Cavalier who can gallop into war; or a Columbine and Harlequin who can turn to each other and away again. It's very rare to find one of these pictures over here, but they can be tracked down in America (although what their current price might be, I have no idea).

As for *musical* dancing dolls—they were fantastic!

France led the way with a series of fairy-tale sequinned creatures dressed in satins and pearls, with real hair; who twizzled around on one leg when the clockwork motors were wound up. There were Harlequins; and single dancing dogs and cats; and singing birds in gilded cages; and circus scenes; and moving orchestras; and crowds of dancing people; who all performed to the strains of Faust or other well-known composers, at the flick of one's fingers. Tiny bellows in the throats of the birds and dolls, made their songs all the more realistic.

Plinkety-plonk pull along French musical toys were made in great quantity too; with Gipsy violinists and dancers who nodded their plumed and hatted heads, and twirled their braided skirts as they were dragged along. (These were often called 'Mobiles'.) All these musical mechanical dolls had porcelain faces and hands and the dancing animals had real fur heads and paws and beautiful clothes straight out of a Court scene at Versailles—all lace and ribbons and gold braiding. They were splendid fantasy toys indeed! But other French clockwork animals were being made too, as real as the dancing musical fantasy animals were not; there was a tiger that could spring and growl, and was 'werry fierce', and there were realistic galloping stallions covered in real skin; and mistrustful-looking dogs who could snarl and show their teeth; and *these* clockwork toys were rather frightening, and brought forth none of the 'oohs' and 'ahs' produced by watching the 'glamour' dolls dance.

In America at this time, similar dolls were being made, but these had a 'homespun' quality about them, which failed to appeal to a market overwhelmed with French ribbons and lace. American dancing dolls wore calico and cotton and woollen shawls. Who could compare them to the dazzling Columbines, even if their mechanical parts were equally inventive? Now, while the females in the family were being entranced by these warbling fantasy toys, great developments were taking place behind the scenes, in the field of toys with sheer *masculine* appeal. Whether the manufacturers aimed at the fathers or the sons it's hard to say, but wherever they aimed, they certainly caught and held all masculine attention with their clockwork and steam toy locomotives; their rolling stocks, and electric miniature trains; and all their inventive and beautifully made accessories.

Steam trains were the first to appear, inspired by Stevenson's 'Rocket' (which can be seen in the London Science Museum); and of course Germany, with her already established tin markets came to the fore at once, and made tin trains a few inches high especially for export to England, with ROCKET painted on the side of the engine, and RAIL ROAD COMPANY on the carriage doors. The carriages were comical things, shaped rather more like the coaches that carried passengers on the roads, than the streamlined coaches the later trains were to boast. Of course, the engines and carriages were modelled in the round, which was an important advance after a history of flat pressed tin toys, and they were coloured carefully by hand. At first these trains were sold without rails, but by 1865, Germany was selling clockwork train 'sets' that included rails as well as passengers, signals, tunnels, and engines.

Steam trains grew bigger, and as they developed their parts were made to be interchangeable with other steam toys; whereas on the early steam models, all tubes had been hand rolled and then soldered into position, and were immovable. (A useful pointer when dating the models.) There was no standard scaling for the trains at all, so some had big wheels and a small funnel, while others had the emphasis the other way round. It was just enough to have movable trains, and it has been quite late in *this* century (certainly after 1930), that scaling became more and more carefully calculated, until nowadays we are able to buy toy

(1) Miniature of Stevenson's 'Rocket'.

(2) Bing model on which the 'Black Prince' toy engine was based, which was subsequently made by Bassett Lowke of Nuremberg in 1902.

trains anywhere that are perfectly scaled to size.

The British firm of Bassett-Lowke commissioned Bing of Nuremberg to 'Anglicise' their designs at the turn of the century, so the rather 'Continental feel' of most German tin trains gave way to designs like the famous 'Black Prince', a splendidly sturdy model with buffers and pistons, and very far removed from the early copies of the 'Rocket', as you can see from the illustration. And during the Edwardian period, urged on by Bassett-Lowke, Bing experimented with mini-railways and achieved great success in 1922 with the first ever workable mini. It went electric two years later and this was eventually followed by 'remote control'. Electricity, using the house supply, or special petrol-driven power plants, had been by then successfully used for about 25 years. The scoop and subsequent publicity for this achievement went to Carette (another Nuremberg firm), so it seems quite plain that although the making of toy trains was certainly not exclusive to Germany, the German attention to detail and design made their products leaders in this field.

In England, Hornby was laying the foundations of a long and successful business; in America the toy trains made of iron (often called 'carpet toys' if they were sold without rails) had a deserved success; and France was becoming famed for producing the cheapest tin trains of all (due to a flourishing cheap tin scrap business in Paris). France did much towards lessening the costs of colouring train sets too, by inventing a 'dyeing' process that involved baking a special varnish paint-mix which contained alcohol. In the heat of the oven, the alcohol burnt away, leaving a thin, hard, translucent coating of colour, and this process was used on all but the most expensive models (which were still hand-painted), in conjunction, around 1900, with colour transfers (which involved a lithographic process). What did a toy railway cost in the late Victorian period? I've been asking a lot of people exactly that—because now, to possess a complete mini-railway (by Bing, for example), one is asked a very great deal of money indeed. Perhaps a hundred pounds if the set is extensive.

But around 1925, catalogues listed locomotives at 3s. each for clockwork, (and 10s. for electric); 6d. for a passenger car; 1s. for an engine shed; 3d. for a telegraph pole; and 1s. for a wayside station, comprising a waiting room on a large portion of platform. Colours were gay, using yellow, red, black, and green; little porters (costing a few pence) were blue; and trees and houses (a few pence to 4s.) green, brown, and scarlet. So for a relatively small outlay, one could build up a bright, beautifully running set that was guaranteed to keep working for years. Larger goods vans (measuring 8 in long) cost about 3s. 6d.; timber trucks ($6\frac{1}{2}$ in long) cost 2s. 6d.; and express passenger coaches (15 in long) cost 15s. 6d., which is quite a lot more; but still, by our reckoning, cheap. To own an electric (or even a clockwork) railway set today is almost a luxury, due to high prices; but it was something most comfortable Victorian families took for granted.

I must admit that due to the expense, we've never actually bought any Victorian or Edwardian toy trains or equipment in our family. You have to draw the line somewhere. And we've a fair collection of other toys, most of which I've already mentioned earlier in the book. But to bring the book to a close, I want to tell you about the toys that give the most pleasure to the family as a whole . . . our collection of 'moving' optical toys . . . our magic lanterns, and our collection of slides themselves.

It all started with a party we planned to give, and to which all our relations were to be invited, including eleven adults and eight children. Space was limited, and it became quite a problem trying to decide what to do with all the aunts and cousins except feed them. I foresaw the party as an endless round of eating and drinking, punctuated; far worse! with an endless round of washing up. 'What we want,' said my sister, 'is an entertainment.' I gloomily assured her that when all the children started fighting, there'd be *plenty* of entertainment . . . but she was not to be put off, and we began to make a list of possible 'fun' things to do. The magic-lantern show idea happened by accident as we wandered aimlessly through the Chelsea Antique Market. (It is absolutely normal for anyone in my family to head for an antique market or shop when there are nerves to be calmed down! Which is probably why we all possess so many antique bits and pieces. The antiques certainly calm our nerves—but they just as certainly burn a hole in our resources!

Anyway, there we were; we stopped to inspect a magic lantern; we paused; exchanged glances; asked with one voice to see it in action; loved it; bought it; and our problem was solved! All in ten minutes flat! What we had bought, was, in fact, a solid late nineteenth-century magic lantern; and with it a wooden box of fifteen assorted glass slides; all for £10. We'd never, consciously, seen one before, and could hardly wait to get it home. It stood squarely on the table, its funnel-like lens poking forward beyond the main structure. Over the lens was a protective cover and screws to adjust the focus. Lighting was to be achieved by oil. The slides were mostly movable, with either a projecting handle on the side to turn in order to get one glass section of the slide to draw across the other; or a fitment to pull across, which achieved the same result. Thus a lion painted on one section of the slide, closed and opened its mouth when the turning handle closed the second section; and little Red Riding Hood took a forward step, when *her* slide was given a sharp pull.

The party entertainment was a great success; and we felt we'd hit on the perfect answer to Christmas and Boxing Days that seem to last three weeks; and boring recuperation days, when one has had 'flu and can't go out. We began to look about for new slides, and for other optical-illusion toys. We found out that the principle behind our particular lantern had been known since the thirteenth century; and that by the seventeenth century public demonstrations were put on in London; where one was even attended by Samuel Pepys (who, you'll recall, loved theatres and puppet shows). At the end of the nineteenth century, candles and oil used to light the earlier lanterns, these gave way to oxy-hydrogen lighting and with this, magic-lantern shows for *large* audiences became a possibility. For these grand shows, two or three lanterns were mounted on top of each other; each with a slide depicting a different view of the same object, which could then present movement and 'fade-outs' quite easily. A few lanterns were made with two or three lenses on the same body (one of these gave a splendid show at the National film theatre recently), and these proved easier to handle.

The magic-lantern became invaluable in the field of education; presenting the moving planets; the techniques of swimming, etc. The nearest 'optical-illusion' toy we bought (for a few shillings in a junk shop), was a Thaumatrope. Thaumatropes work on the principle that the eye retains (on the retina) an impression of the object it has just seen, although the object has been withdrawn. The impression only lasts a moment, but if the first object has been rapidly replaced by object number two, a sort of optical 'overlap' results. For example, with a bird sitting on a branch, or a cup sitting on a saucer. Although the bird and the cup have been shown and removed, and have been replaced by the branch and the saucer, one 'sees' the objects together.

In construction the Thaumatrope couldn't be simpler. It consists of a disc, on one side of which is drawn the cup, and the other, its related object, the saucer. On either side of the disc is a loop. You simply hold the loops and twirl the disc, and hey presto! there is the saucer holding its cup in perfect position. A modern version of this toy is the little gold charm that is made to dangle on a bracelet. Both sides are engraved with a few hieroglyphics that turn into the words 'I love you' when the charm is spun. (I've got one from Italy that says 'te amo'.)

Zoetropes take this principle further (and nearer to modern day cinemas), by spinning a role of pin figures, all slightly different from the figure before; inside a drum. You look through slits in the drum, and fancy the pin-figures move. (You can get the same result by drawing pin figures on the corners of each page in a book, and then flicking the pages.) The Zoetrope I finally bought, I found in a shop in the mountains near Milan in Italy, which seemed to stock entirely English Victoriana! I climbed over the button-backed chairs and the Rockingham china, and pounced on the metal Zoetrope! Its heavy base was damaged, but the drum itself was in good shape, and there was a lovely set of paper rolls to go with it. Most of them involve the antics of a frog playing ball, which is highly amusing! And there's a jack-in-the-box who peeps out, more, more, and more, and finally pops right out; and a series of sailing ships; seagulls; moon risings; and sun settings. (This particular toy has been marvellous for small children's tea-parties, and the children can even make their own pin-figure strips to use—which they adore doing!)

The machine I'm searching for now, is a Praxinoscope—a machine even more closely related to the cinema which was invented in 1878 by the Frenchman, Emile Reynaud. This, like the Zoetrope, depends on a band of pin-figures; but here, the figures revolve around a central set of mirrors, and their reflections in the mirrors are projected by further mirrors and lenses on to a screen. Sometimes a static scene is painted on this screen, so that one gets the optical illusion of moving people against, for example, a beautiful garden.

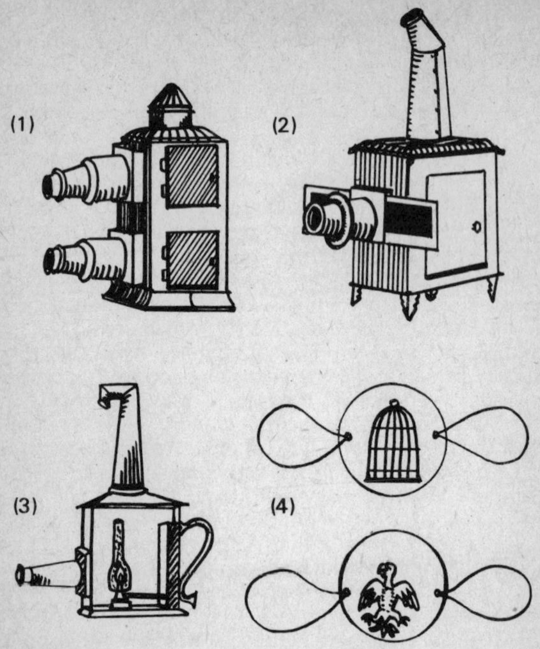

(1) A Bi-Unial Lantern which can project two slides at one time.

(2) An 'optical lantern' made by Bing in 1890.

(3) A simple slide lantern, drawn to show the typical lamp system used inside.

(4) A thaumatrope, showing both sides. When spun by the loops, the bird appears to sit inside the cage.

(5) A Zoetrope. A strip, 6, is placed inside; the zoetrope is spun, and seen through the slits, the strip appears as a moving picture.

What further developments took place in the field of optical toys would make a complete story all of its own. It includes the invention of flexible transparent film and Kinetoscopes; and involves great inventors like Friese-Greene and Rudge. With it is tangled the story of photography, and that, in its turn, is involved with the story of Art, and the new techniques required of artists once photographs took part of their bread and butter from them. And if you delve further into these stories, and other stories surrounding the whole fascination of playthings, you'll find yourself an unbeatable interest and hobby, as I've done.

CHAPTER NINE

TOY MUSEUMS, BOOKS, AND CLUBS

To study *outdoor* games, played with vigour by people *of* all ages, *in* all ages; like knuckle bones (five stones); hopscotch; football; and golf; you must study old manuscripts and paintings; and even Classical ceramics.

But *indoor* games have been lovingly collected and housed in museums, and here's a list of the museums I've enjoyed the most.

In Holland
Wonderful seventeenth- and eighteenth-century dolls' houses in the

  (1) *Rijksmuseum, Amsterdam*—and—nothing at all to do with dolls—if you go to the Rijksmuseum, please see the Meissen collection!

In the U.S.A.
  (1) Dolls in the *City Museum, New York*—and in Philadelphia, the only Antique Toy Collector's club I came across—with some very enthusiastic supporters.

In Great Britain
  (1) *The Rottingdean Toy Museum*, the Grange, Rottingdean, near Brighton, for small toys, games, and dolls.
  (2) *Bethnal Green Museum*, and the *London Museum*, London.

(3) *The Edinburgh Museum of Childhood*—full of fascinating facts and examples.
(4) *Pollock's Toy Museum*, Scala Street, London W.1. (also a shop).
(5) *The Tollcross Children's Museum* at Glasgow, which has a good doll collection.
(6) *Bromsgrove 'Playthings Past Museum'* in Worcestershire.
(7) *The Abbey House Museum in Leeds*, where there are eighteenth-century harpsichord dolls that dance.
(8) *The Pump Room at Harrogate* (a lovely town!)
(9) *The Royal Tunbridge Wells Museum* at the Civic Centre, where there are dolls and toys of all kinds.
(10) *The Somerset County Museum* at Taunton Castle.
(11) *The Rotunda, 44 Iffley Turn, Oxford*, dolls' houses 1700–1885.
(12) *Snowshill Manor* in the delightful village of Broadway.
(13) *Looe, Cornwall*, pastimes and games (*and* relics of witchcraft!)
(14) *Asreton Manor* in the Isle of Wight.

This list does not include *all* museums with toys and dolls; in fact new collections are being formed all the time, which is splendid. This is just a list of museums I, personally, have enjoyed. You'll see that the museums are to be found in all corners of England and Scotland, and even on the pretty little Isle of Wight, so there's no excuse for not following up any growing interest you may have developed on the subject. A more comprehensive list can be found in *Museums and Galleries, Great Britain and Ireland*, published, at around 50 new pence, annually, by INDEX publications, and found in most bookshops.

Other useful and interesting books—again, ones *I've* specially enjoyed out of a very large range available—are the following:

(1) *Dolls of the World*, by Gwen White—a 'must' if dolls are your delight.
(2) *How to Repair and Dress Old Dolls*, by A. Johnson—full of interesting and practical information.
(3) *Punch and Judy*, by George Speight, who also wrote
(4) *The History of the English Toy Theatre*. Both published by Studio Vista, and essential for everyone interested in the field of entertainment.
(5) *English Dolls' Houses*, by V. Greene, with some nice illustrations.
(6) *Children's Toys throughout the Ages*, by L. Daikin, which gives fascinating glimpses of past history.
(7) *An Illustrated History of Toys*, by Fritzsch-Bachmann. Published by Abbey Library, this gives the most detail on German toys found anywhere.

Any librarian will supplement this necessarily short list with other suggestions. But these should keep you busy—and happy—for quite a while!

And as a final word: The *Daily Telegraph* lists all important forthcoming auctions (for everything antique), in its Monday editions. Good doll sales are *always* listed.

CORGI MINI-BOOKS

continued

☐	76046 3	HOUSEWORK—THE EASY WAY		
		Claire Rayner, S.R.N.	12½p
☐	76318 7	HANDWRITING Dorothy Sara	12½p
☐	76380 2	SEX AND MARRIAGE Margaret Smyth	17½p
☐	76386 1	FAMILY PLANNING Margaret Smyth	17½p
☐	76374 8	SLIM THE FRENCH WAY Jean Soward	17½p
☐	76347 0	SHAPE UP TO BEAUTY Helen Speed	15p
☐	76390 X	HOW TO TRACE YOUR ANCESTORS
		Dr. John Tanner	17½p
☐	76378 0	DISH GARDENS, JUNGLE JARS AND
		PUDDLE POTS Violet Stevenson	17½p
☐	76376 4	UPHOLSTERY AND SOFT FURNISHINGS
		V. J. Taylor	17½p
☐	76053 6	THE THOUGHTFUL GIFT BUYER'S GUIDE
		Roma Thewes	12½p
☐	76322 5	NAME YOUR SON Roma Thewes	15p
☐	76323 3	NAME YOUR DAUGHTER Roma Thewes	15p
☐	76057 9	HOMEMADE WINE Rex Tremlett	15p
☐	76097 8	CREAM WITH EVERYTHING Lorna Walker	12½p
☐	76361 6	COLLECTING SILVER AND PLATE
		Guy Williams	15p
☐	76357 8	COLLECTING VICTORIANA Guy Williams	15p
☐	76049 8	DESIGN GUIDE TO HOME DECORATING
		Guy Williams	12½p
☐	76321 7	COLLECTING CHEAP CHINA AND GLASS
		Guy Williams	12½p
☐	76356 X	PALMISTRY (illustrated) Joyce Wilson	15p
☐	76384 5	POT OR NOT? A. J. Wood	17½p
☐	76316 0	DOWN LEFT WITH FEELING—THE UNPAID
		ACTOR'S HANDBOOK John Woodnutt	12½p
☐	76328 4	A CAREER FOR YOUR SON Henry Woolland	12½p
☐	76345 4	THE MAGIC OF HERBS Audrey Wynne-Hatfield	15p

All these books are available at your local bookshop or newsagent; or can be ordered direct from the publisher. Just tick the titles you want and fill in the form below.

CORGI BOOKS, Cash Sales Department, P.O. Box 11, Falmouth, Cornwall.
Please send cheque or postal order. No currency, and allow 4p per book to cover the cost of postage and packing in U.K., 6p per copy overseas.

NAME ....

ADDRESS ....

....